The Case of the "HOPELESS" Marriage

A Nouthetic Counseling Case from Beginning to End

JAY E. ADAMS

with Greg Dawson and Bert and Sue Lancaster

TIMELESS TEXTS
STANLEY, NC

INTRODUCTION

A Counseling Case (Exhibited)

Chapter twenty of my book *How to Help People in Conflict: Becoming a Biblical Peacemaker* was devoted to one slimmed-down simulated counseling session. The sort of interest in this chapter that some have shown makes me think that a volume in which I set forth an entire case in a similar manner might be useful to biblical counselors. I know of nothing like it in nouthetic circles. Hence, this book.

The case I have chosen is typical of many you will encounter. It is a composite based upon a number of those in which, over the years, I have counseled husbands and wives about their marriages. Every counselor knows that on the list of counseling problems marriage and family difficulties rank #1. That is the reason for beginning with a case of the sort.[1] Having counseled two hours a day, two days a week, for several years, I think that I can fairly exhibit the sorts of things that husbands and wives do and say, as well as how counselors must respond. The case in this book lasts for ten weekly sessions,[2] which I have found is a common length of time for marriage counseling of this nature (note the word "common").

The case presented presupposes several factors that you should know before launching into the book itself. (If you are one who doesn't read introductions to books, you will be at a loss unless you read this one.) Sue, a 38-year old mother of two small children (Billy and Tommy), and Bert, a 42-year old civil engineer, have come to Greg, their pastor, for help. Their marriage is falling apart. They joined the "First Scrip-

---

1. If this book is generally well-received, it is possible that I shall publish others dealing with different sorts of cases.
2. Plus a six-week checkup. For details about this, see *Critical Stages of Biblical Counseling*, the third stage of which deals with termination. My hope is that, in the present book, I shall be able to show you how the principles found in the above referenced book work out in actual practice.

tural Presbyterian Church"[1] two years ago. Both were converted under the evangelistic efforts of one of the church's elders. They have been faithful members ever since. It was, therefore, something of a surprise to Greg to hear that they had called the church for a counseling appointment.

Immediately, the first available time was set for a meeting, which happened to be Monday evening at 7:30PM. When they arrived at 7:00PM, as arranged, the secretary greeted them, showed them to a quiet room, and gave each a copy of the *Personal Data Inventory* to fill out.[2] These forms were completed by 7:20PM; the secretary then took them to the pastor's study for his perusal.

Upon receiving their PDIs, Pastor Greg scanned their answers to the initial questions (some of the factual data he already knew – address, phone number, etc.). He circled a couple of items he thought it might be necessary to gather further information about. Then, he turned to the last page. At this point, we shall take up the case.

Jay Adams

---

1. I hope that by inventing this fictional denomination I have not unknowingly stepped on anyone's feet! I tried to call it by a name that – so far as I know – doesn't exist. Incidentally, all names and places in this book are likewise fictional and apply to no known persons walking on the face of the earth.
2. Copies of the PDI may be found in *The Christian Counselor's Manual.*

THE BEGINNING...

As he surveyed the answers to the four basic questions on the last page of the PDI, Greg came to some initial, but tentative, conclusions. In addition, there arose in his mind some important questions. Here is what he read.[1]

BERT'S PDI

1. What is your problem (as you see it)?

We have trouble getting along.

2. What have you done about it?

What *can* I do? She won't listen to me. Everything I say is wrong. What have I *done?* Well, I've tried all sorts of things, but *nothing* I do seems to help. I'm always wrong, no matter what I do or say. We just can't go on this way any longer.

3. What do you want us to do?

I have no idea. You tell me what to do.

4. Is there anything else we should know?

No.

SUE'S PDI

1. What is your problem (as you see it)?

We are not compatible. Over the years of our marriage, I've done everything I know to make a go of it, but Bert simply won't try to make things better. He seems to think that

---

1. For convenience, I shall list Sue and Bert's PDI answers one at a time. In his mind, among other things, Greg compared and contrasted their words. Periodically I will interrupt the conversation with running commentary on what Greg thought and, as the session proceeds, what he learned from it. I shall also comment on what he said and did. This basic plan is used throughout the book. It is my hope that the discussions will prove valuable. I shall attempt to keep them, as much as possible, from interrupting the flow of counseling.

I'm to blame for everything. I don't think he loves me any more – if he ever did!!!

The psychologist that I saw two years ago said that not only are we incompatible, but also that there is no hope for our marriage. He thought that I'd be better off if I got out of it. Probably he was right.

Bert never talks to me. When he does, we usually get into a fight. I don't even know why we're here – things are so hopeless!!!

2. What have you done about it?

When all else failed, I went to see a marriage and family counselor. I told you what he said.

I'm sure that Bert wants to end the marriage, but I guess he's afraid to do it – probably because of alimony and so forth.

I didn't think that divorce was a possibility until a friend recently gave me a copy of an old article by Dr. James Dobson entitled, "Husband Who Feels Suffocated Needs To Be Set Free."[1] He says that I can "open the cage door" and let my husband go free!!! Maybe that's the best thing to do. I've attached a copy of the article to this Inventory.

3. What do you want us to do?

Who knows? You're the doctor! I guess what I want most of all is for us to be able to talk civilly. Tell me whether there is any hope at all. And if not, help us to get a divorce that isn't as bloody and miserable as most of them are. If there were any hope, I'd say, "help us to make a go of our marriage," but I think it's too far gone. After all, how can two persons as incompatible as we are ever get along?

4. Is there anything else we should know?

No. I've said it all.

---

1. Spartanburg Herald-Journal, August 26, 1998. Online at http://www.uexpress.com/focusonthefamily/index.html?uc_full_date=20011111.

Let's pause for a moment to discuss their answers on the PDIs...

Note the brevity of Bert's answers. Is he embarrassed? Does he really care about the marriage – about Sue? Is he simply the non-communicative type? Has he given up? In response to question #2, he opens up a bit. It seems that he might want to preserve the marriage, but hasn't the faintest idea what to do. Why is he here? To please Sue? To get help? To find a way out of the marriage? There is lots of uncertainty about Bert.

In contrast, look at Sue's more detailed responses. If she thinks there's no hope, why is she here? Is it because there's a lingering remnant of hope? Is this her last effort to save the marriage? Does she agree with the psychologist? She didn't take his advice, yet keeps on mentioning what he said. She probably got the idea of "incompatibility" from him. Greg thinks, "At some point will I have to take on what the psychologist said?"

Her exclamation points probably indicate strong emotion. Is she more angry with Bert than anything else? She has been steered in the wrong direction by the psychologist, and now that I glance over the newspaper article, I must conclude also by Dobson. Why did she give me a copy of his article? To convince me of his views? To get my take on it? While she failed to take his advice, she remembers it. Is she ready to get out of the marriage at last unless I can show her some hope? Is she here to try to make up her mind?

Greg is thinking well about what he read. He has used their answers productively to stimulate his thinking. He probably scribbled some of his tentative thoughts on his *Weekly Counseling Record*.[1] Then, at the appropriate time, he will return to these notes. Of utmost importance: he will find it necessary to give much hope to each of these counselees.

---

1. A copy of this sheet may be found in *The Christian Counselor's Manual*. The agenda column is especially helpful in assisting counselors to recall items that they might otherwise forget.

Their marriage seems in *serious* danger at this point. If he fails in his counseling, it will probably break up. We must await to see what he does.

Greg must form a plan in his mind about how best to proceed. One thing that he usually does will work well here: he will begin with comments about, and ask further questions concerning, the responses that Bert and Sue have written to the basic PDI questions just listed. How they respond to *him* as he does so, will provide additional clues about Bert and Sue. He should be listening and looking[1] carefully to see what comes next. He has evaluated them only on paper thus far; now he must consider them as talking, responding persons. Will they come across differently or not? Chances are that there will be some consistencies and some inconsistencies. Noting what these are may be of significance in any such evaluation.

Now, we shall listen in on the conversation.

---

1. Halo data (some call "body language") may be of importance as well as words.

SESSION ONE

Pastor: It's good to see you. Please sit down. I'm glad you came here before you made any rash decisions. I want you to know that I'll work with you for as long as necessary to help you solve your problems. And – let me say at the outset – they *can* be solved. I say that because you're both Christians. That means that you have newness of life to enable you to do God's will, you have the Bible to direct you how to do it, and you have God's Spirit to strengthen and help you do it.

Sue: I wish I were as certain about that as you are, pastor.

Bert: Yeah, me too.

Pastor: Well, we'll see. Now, let me ask you a few questions. I'm not sure about your comments here on the PDI, Sue. Have you given up hope, or did you come here hoping there would be some solution to your problems? Your remarks seem to waver back and forth about this.

Sue: Well, I guess you're right. I'm just undecided – about almost everything.

Pastor: That's good in one sense: it means that you're still willing to look into possibilities. Your mind isn't made up then – right?

Sue: Mmmm...I guess not. But I know which way I'm leaning.

Pastor: Which way is that?

Sue: Unless you can work some magic, I'm thinking of divorcing him.

Pastor: I see. Well, we'll have to talk about that. But for now, just let me say this: I've got something better than magic to offer you! Bert, let me ask you as well – what you want to do?

Bert: It should be obvious. With her I haven't a chance – she's *leaning* toward a divorce she says. How do you like that?

7

Pastor: Not too much. But Bert, I asked you about yourself, not about Sue. What do you want?

Bert: I don't know what I want. One day I want her to leave; then the next day I can't even think about living without her. It isn't easy to decide what to do.

Pastor: I see. It sounds then like you're uncertain too. Again, let me stress that this is good. It means that you haven't yet come to any hard decisions.

Bert: I guess not.

Pastor: Okay, thank you both for your comments. Now, let me explain a few things. I've already said that as Christians it's always possible to solve problems if you are willing to do so. But that's true only *if* you follow God's directions in His Word. No matter how bad the marriage is right now, I *guarantee* that God will give you a marriage that sings if you follow His directions! But it *will* take doing what He says. I can say this because God has promised that…

Sue [breaking in]: That sounds good and all that, but if you knew our circumstances…

Pastor: Sue, I don't need to know them in order to know God's promises. All I have to know is what God says…

Bert: What *does* He say?

Pastor: I was just about to tell you. Listen to this verse: "No trial has taken hold of you except that which other people have experienced; but God is faithful Who will not allow you to be tried beyond what you are able to bear, but rather, will provide together with the trial the way out so that you may be able to endure it." That's I Corinthians 10:13.

Sue: Sounds good, but our case is unique. If you only knew what I have to put up with…

Bert: [breaking in] What *you* have to put up with? Why you…Pastor, let me tell you what living with that woman is like. She…

Pastor: Now, please…wait a minute. We'll get nowhere if you start quarreling. If you have anything to say, I suggest that you say it to me, not to one another. You don't know how to talk to each other yet. As a part of our counseling, eventually you'll have to learn to do so. But for now, talk to me instead. Okay?

Sue and Bert [mumbling]: I suppose so [and] Yeah.

Pastor: And while we're at it, let me suggest that you'll want to be careful about your language. We'll talk as Christians should during these sessions, even if that's the only time when you talk properly all week long. If we want to get somewhere in counseling, there can be no fighting or nasty talking. Now, let me explain that verse.

Let's pause for a moment to discuss what's happened so far…

Greg seems to be doing well so far. Primarily, he has been doing three things. 1) He has been attempting to discover how far gone the marriage is. It looks like it's in a very serious condition, but not hopeless. It's going to take "some doing" to pull it out! 2) He has been giving some hope initially, so far only with general assurances. (It looks like he'll go on with this when he explains I Corinthians 10:13.) In quoting the verse and explaining it, he will be asserting God's authority. He will want their hope to rest on *that*; not on Greg's word alone. 3) And he has been setting out some rules for counseling. By doing this, he has taken control of the session, not allowing it to get out of hand. He's setting up conditions for future sessions as well as for this one. That's crucial if he's going to get anywhere. Patterns for counseling will be set early on, so they should be good ones from the beginning (indeed, from the first session), not something you drift into that you will have to change in days to come.

It looks, then, as if Greg is on track since he has begun to do the three most fundamental things that a counselor should work on in a first session: basic data gathering, giving a reason to hope, setting the rules for counseling.

What is Greg thinking? He's thinking, "They're really in bad shape. I hope they'll hang in there. Right now, it seems touch-and-go. I don't want to lose them. It *does* seem as if they haven't made up their minds – that's good! If all goes well and they do what God says, I guess that this case will last for at least eight to ten weeks. That is, if they stick to counseling. It seems that they aren't *too* feisty, but I'll have to watch out for changes and work hard at making sure they're not merely holding back. Oh Lord, help me and help them to bring honor to Your Name out of this mess. Now, I'm going to try to strengthen their hope."

Let's continue…

Pastor: As I said, God makes some wonderful promises to His children – promises that you can bank on. In I Corinthians 10:13, Paul says three things: In effect, he tells you, Sue, that your situation isn't unique – God has helped others to go through similar trials successfully. And he then goes on to say that God is faithful in not allowing anything to come your way that is more than you can bear, *if* you handle it His way. I know that may at first seem unrealistic to you, but Paul has assured us that this promise is based on God's faithfulness. That means it can't fail. And finally, Paul assures us that He will show the way out of the problem. There is hope. Notice how he stresses the faithfulness of God. If any of these promises should fail, God would no longer be God. Paul is saying that you can count on them. God doesn't fail to keep His promises. Before you leave, I'm going to give you a little booklet that will explain this verse even further.[1] Well, what do you think about what the verse says? Is it helpful? Doesn't it encourage you?

Sue: I don't know…

---

1. That is the pamphlet, *Christ and Your Problems.*

10

Pastor: Do you doubt God's Word?

Sue: No, it's not that but… [she is at a loss for words, and when she pauses, Bert chimes in].

Bert: I can understand why Sue said that. It's hard to believe that after all we've been through we could ever pull this marriage out of the fire.

Sue: [just a bit appreciative that Bert has saved her from saying something she'd regret]: Yeah, Bert's right. It seems unreal. Are you sure that the promises in this verse are for us, pastor?

Pastor: Absolutely! And they aren't the only ones I could quote. But they're more than enough for now. After all, if God says something once, that's it. We don't need to pile up verses to be sure of His Word. Now, let's gather some more data about your situation. Bert, what would you say is the main problem? I noticed that on your Personal Data Inventory you were just a bit vague about it.

Bert: Well, we haven't been getting along for some time now. It seems that she won't let me be the head of the house. I…

Sue: Won't let you? When did you ever try? You know full well that you…

Pastor: Now, Sue, please let Bert finish. Your turn will come soon enough. We can't all talk at once. And I'd appreciate it if you addressed me – as we agreed – rather than arguing with Bert. Now, Bert, go on.

Bert: Well, as I was saying – before she flew into one of her tirades…

Sue: See, pastor, he can't be civil. A tirade? Hummph!

Pastor: Sue, you simply must not interrupt. But I am glad you addressed me this time instead of Bert. Thanks! And Bert, be careful how you say things. There's no need for inflammatory language. Go on, Bert.

Bert: As I was trying to say before she…

Pastor: Be careful Bert.

Bert: Okay. Okay. As I was saying, every time I try to assume my duty as the head of my home, Sue undermines me. She always knows better. She always has another way. She always contradicts me. The kids don't know who to believe.

Pastor: Now let me get this straight. This *always* happens? That sounds like a bit of an overstatement.

Bert: Well, it happens a lot, anyway.

Pastor: That's better. You see, when you use exaggerated language, you not only irritate other people who can then argue that what you say is inaccurate, but you also tend to convince yourself as well. We usually come to believe what we say often enough – whether it's true or not. Now, tell me, what do you mean by "assuming your duties as head of the house."

Bert: Making decisions, of course. Using my God-given authority to tell the rest of the family what to do.

Pastor: I see. And what do you base that understanding of headship upon?

Let's pause to discuss…

Clearly, Greg has gotten into the thick of things by now. He is beginning to see how things go on in their home. Everything negative that he sees and hears here, he should mentally multiply by a factor of at least five. People are usually more restrained in another person's presence.

Even though they argue and contradict one another, by comparison with some cases Greg's had, they still don't seem all that feisty. They haven't turned on him, and their objections are reasonably mild. Greg will probably have little trouble training them how to talk over the next session or two, if not sooner.

Now, what's going on? Greg is trying to understand what their situation at home is like. And he wants to know something of the nub of the problem. He is trying to get Bert's view on matters, but Sue keeps on interrupting. He has promised her time in the future to speak, hoping that will keep her quiet for the moment so he can hear what Bert is trying to say.

You will notice that Greg has established God's Word as the standard for what will go on in counseling. It is His promises that everyone is to depend on, not on Greg's assurances. And what God says in I Corinthians 10:13 is most emphatic. He even stakes His own reputation – His faithfulness – on carrying through what He has promised. That's a sure foundation on which to base all Greg's counseling to come.

Because they only mildly object that possibly they are an exception, Sue and Bert seem to accept God's Word for what it is. That's encouraging. They will need an explanation of how those promises might take place in their situation, it's true, but they seem to be willing to hear, in spite of these mild objections.

Also notice that Bert "saved" Sue from having to say whether or not she doubts God's Word. When he did, she looked at him with a measure of appreciation, and you could hear it in her voice. That was a small note of encouragement for Greg: he could see some concern for each other in it. He may be able to build on this in days to come.

But now, he is still in the process of establishing rules: no interruptions, no nasty talk. It seems that Sue is at least beginning to learn to talk to him rather than to Bert, and he commends her for it.

What is Greg thinking?

Well, it's going to take a while to get anything out of Bert, it seems, if Sue keeps on breaking in whenever he tries to talk. I've got to be firm about the rules I've set down. Bert is beginning to explain that he wants to be the head of his home. That's right. And I should commend him for it. But his view of headship seems woefully deficient. He's focused on authority alone. I'm going to have to get him to think biblically about it. So far as I can see at this point, he seems to want to be a little Hitler. Since both Bert and Sue seem to respect God's authority, I'll point them to some significant passages on the subject. But, because I have an entire sermon about headship, I'll have to be careful not to turn it into a half-hour lecture.

Let's continue…

Pastor: Bert, it's good that you want to be the head of your home. But let's think for a moment about headship as God talks about it. To begin with, in Ephesians 5:23, Paul says that the husband is to be the "head of his wife *as Christ also is head of the church.*" How do you interpret that verse?

Bert: That I'm to run things just as Christ runs the church.

Pastor: I see. Well there are various ways of running things, aren't there? There's the way Saddam Hussein ran Iraq. That's surely not the way you want to run your home, is it?

Bert: Well, ugh…No I guess it isn't. But headship does mean being in charge.

Pastor: Right. But here it says that husbands are to exercise headship *the way* Christ does. How do you think He does that? Isn't it different from a dictator's way of running things?

Bert: Well, sure, but…

Pastor: Good. Glad you see that. Here's how it differs: Paul tells us that Jesus is "Head over all things *for the sake of the church*" (Ephesians 1:22). Everything He does, He does for the church's benefit. He even put the church before His own interests in coming to die for her. Now that's a special kind of headship, isn't it?

Bert: I suppose so.

Pastor: Think for a moment about what that means. What did Christ do for His church? He loved her and gave Himself for her. Surely, love is a prime ingredient of headship; one that you seem to have missed. Am I right about that?

Bert: Well, possibly. I suppose so, but I can't die for her sins the way Christ did.

Pastor: Of course not. But the principle of loving your wife as much as Christ loved the church still remains. Paul continues, "Husbands, love your wives just as Christ loved the church and gave Himself up for her" (Ephesians 5:25). And according to Philippians 2, He put her interests before His own.[1] Can you see that?

Bert: Mmmm. Yeah.

Pastor: You seem uncertain.

Bert: It's just that if she'd listen to me, I could love her more.

Pastor: Whoa! Did Christ's love depend on our love for Him? Didn't He love us in spite of the fact that we were sinners — even enemies? We weren't listening to *Him*.

Bert: Okay. Okay. Go on. I guess I'm learning something.

Pastor: Great! Now listen to this "We [the church] love because He [Jesus] *first* loved us." (I John 4:19). That's powerful stuff!

Sue: See, I told him! He should love me by putting me first.

Pastor: Although you happen to be right, Sue, you've interrupted again. He needed to hear *God* tell him so in His Word. What you or I say is relatively unimportant. And let me assure you, we shall get to *your* responsibilities in a matter of time.

Bert: Tell her, pastor!

Pastor: Now, Bert…

---

1. If necessary, Greg might have had to show how Philippians 2:3 is illustrated by the kenosis passage that follows it.

Bert: Okay, okay.

Pastor: If you want to be the head of your home, you must be willing to lead your wife and children by your love for them. Fundamental to headship is *loving leadership.* Did you know that there isn't a single word in the Bible that commands a woman to love her husband?[1] Of course, it's okay for wives to do so! But, every *command* to love in a marriage is given to the husband. If a home lacks love, therefore, that's the husband's fault. How does that grab you, Bert?

Bert: Wow! I guess it hits me right in the head. I suppose I've got to spend time letting that percolate.

Pastor: Not a bad idea.

Bert: But if that's so, what does it mean – that I'm to go about being mushy all the time? That I'm to give in to her every whim?

Pastor: No. You've raised some important questions. Let me answer them. First, in the Bible love isn't the same as feeling. Hollywood and the TV have led us astray. It isn't oceans of emotions. Nor is it the way two people sin in the back seat of a car. It is giving. If you get anything out of this discussion, I hope you get that – love is giving! Listen to this: John 3:16 says, "God so loved the world that He gave...." Galatians 2:20 says, He "loved me and gave Himself up for me...." Ephesians 5:25 says, "Husbands love your wives just as Christ loved the church and gave Himself up for her." You see, the Bible treats love as giving, not as emoting or "mush." Jesus didn't get all mushy over us; He *died* for us! That's important to recognize. You won't always feel mushy, but you can always give, whether you feel like it or not. Giving doesn't depend on feelings. You can even love an "enemy" by *giving* him something to eat or drink. The point is that you show love to another by giving something that he or she needs that

---

1. The passage in Titus 2:4 is no exception. The word in the KJV translated "love" is really "show affection for." It is a different word entirely.

you have. One way for you to learn to love Sue as you should is to discover what it is that she really needs that you can give to her. That may take time to discover. But we can go to work on it. I know a couple of things right off – you can give her time, interest, concern, and help. These generalities must, of course, be translated into concrete acts of love. We'll also get to that in time. Well, I've been giving you a mini-sermon it seems. What do you think?

Bert: It all seems to make sense.

Pastor: Of course it does. That's because it's what God says about love. And when you begin to show love that way, you're going to get a hearing at home. You'll establish as your own the rightful sort of authority that God requires – submission by everyone in the home. We can talk later about what submission is, if you wish to. People *respond* to true love. Remember I John 4:19: our love was generated by Jesus' prior love for us.

[Here the pastor pauses, not saying anything else. The dead air that follows gives everyone time to think.]

Sue: [speaking cautiously] You know, it would be great to live with a husband like that!

Pastor: Of course it would, and there's no reason why Bert can't become such a husband!

Sue: Do you really think it's possible?

Pastor: What do you say, Bert?

Bert: Well, I guess I'd like to be one, but I don't know that I have it in me.

Pastor: Of course you don't have it in you unaided, but God can work in you everything you need to bring it off. Listen to this word to believers, "it is God Who is producing in you both the willingness and the ability to do the things that please Him" (Philippians 2:13). You don't have to pull it off on your own!

17

Bert: Hmmmmm. Whad'yuh think about that, Sue?

Sue: I could live with a husband like that! [Here Greg let her answer his question, even though it was addressed to her instead of to himself. He understands when to be flexible and when not to be.]

Pastor: Sure. I'm sure you could. But you could also live with one *not* like that – if necessary – because, remember, God says that you can bear up under any trial He sends your way. What *you* do doesn't depend on what Bert does or doesn't do. It depends on you. You're responsible for your responses, whether or not you are responding to good or poor treatment. Others can present an occasion for your response, but cannot cause it. But – and this is the point – praise the Lord, you *can* have a husband like that. It'll take time, but perhaps less than you think.

Sue: We'll see.

Pastor: Bert, do you want to become a husband who shows the kind of loving headship that Jesus exemplifies? By His grace (i.e., help) you can, you know.

Bert: Sure. Who wouldn't, but I don't know how Sue would respond. She says it would be great to live with that kind of husband, but the proof of the pudding is in the eating. Would she encourage me or would she still carp away at my failings?

Pastor: Bert, in one respect, it doesn't matter what Sue does or doesn't do. You are to be that kind of husband, not because of how Sue may react, but because God requires it and you want to please Him. A prime principle that you both need to learn is to sort out your responsibilities. You must do what you do, not because of how others respond, but because you want to please God. You are responsible for your own actions. And you must respond biblically regardless of what others do or say. After all, your "peace and joy" don't depend on others – they come from God. I'll write out a key verse that makes this clear. That way you can read together when you go home. [Greg writes out Romans 14:17 and concludes] You'll notice from this verse that – ultimately – peace and joy, as well as righteous living, depend on the Holy Spirit, not on you. He can enable you to have both. And He doesn't fail.

Let's pause to discuss…

Teaching time! That's what you've been listening to. Greg caught their interest when he talked about different kinds of leadership. He got Bert to admit that he didn't want to be running the show the way a dictator does. And that he'd like to become God's kind of husband. From there on, Greg was able to launch a lesson on what true headship involves. He focused on love – something that Bert had no idea was a part of headship. Moreover, he taught both Bert and Sue some biblical facts that most likely surprised them. Especially, about whose responsibility it is to engender and maintain love in the home. Neither one could resist the tidal wave of Bible truth that he unleashed, it seems. Indeed, Sue (at least) seemed to almost revel in the prospect of a loving husband who would put her first. And even Bert had to admit it would be good. But he is still dubious about whether he "has it in him." The pastor tried to head off any such objection by admitting he didn't. But he also said God could make him that kind of person. Greg is getting somewhere. Just to get such a hearing is progress.

In the discussion, Greg was also able to make the crucial point that responsibility to God doesn't depend on what others do or say. And he applied I Corinthians 10:13 to Sue in such a way that made it clear that being a responsible wife, and peace and joy in life, don't depend on others. Greg is making remarkable progress. Will it continue?

Yes, if Greg can keep going as he has, and if Bert and Sue don't hit a snag. Now that he's on a roll, should Greg push further? For instance, should he ask Bert to make a commitment to become the husband God wants him to be? If he did so, he could be forcing him into a commitment that he could not sincerely mean at this time. Would it be better to wait?

Probably. But then, again, there are ways of doing this that may avoid the issue of hypocrisy. Can you think of some?

As well as adding love to Bert's idea of a husband's headship (after subtracting his erroneous concept), Greg was able to define biblical love in a way that both could understand, learn, and practice in days to come. This teaching is invaluable to anyone, whether in a marriage or not. The idea that love is giving will probably come up again in sessions ahead.

Are things going too well? It seems that they are progressing at a steady, but slow pace. Probably, at this point, there is nothing wrong with the progress made. It seems genuine. But note, what they wrote on their PDIs about having no hope has all but disappeared from their talk. Instead, they seem to be toying with the possibility of a marriage that really is God-honoring and a blessing to themselves. Will they revert after the first big brawl when they go home?

You can see one thing, can't you? Greg has succeeded – at least for the moment – in giving them some hope. This session has been long, but seemingly productive. It seems, therefore, important to close it soon. And there is homework yet to be given.

Let's continue…

Pastor: Sue, I promised you that I would give you ample time to tell me what you have in mind. I appreciate it that you have allowed Bert to talk without interruption. Now, our time is growing short, and we have other things to do before you leave, so I believe in order to give you plenty of opportunity, we ought to wait until next week's session to let you do so. I promise that you may have as much time as you want. How about it, Sue? It's up to you.

Sue: Well, this session has been upsetting. I'm not sure of anything any more. It would be good for me to gather my thoughts this week so I can speak logically when we meet next. I think you're right. It would be best to wait rather than to be hasty.

Pastor: Fine. Now, for your homework.

Bert: Homework?

Pastor: Yes. After every session, you'll leave here with something to do at home. In that way two things will happen. It will save us time; counseling won't last so long. And you will be able to put what you learned into practice during the week. As a matter of fact, it's the homework that really solidifies the changes in thinking that may occur in counseling sessions. Got it?

Sue: I guess it makes sense. But what should we do this week?

Pastor: I'll write it out here on this sheet. That way you won't be so likely to forget it, especially if you put it where you'll see it each day. Some people, for instance, like to post it on the bathroom mirror. At any rate, here's what I want you to do. [He writes out the assignment, and as he does so, reads it aloud to them.]:

1. Each of you is to compose a list of 100 or more ways that you are failing God as a person, as a husband or wife, and as a father or mother. I say 100 because that way, we'll get some concrete material. Few people can come up with 100 generalizations. And, people change by doing specific, concrete things, not by "generally" trying to be different in the abstract. Write out your lists, and when you've finished draw a line and then hand the lists to one another to add anything that may be missing. List specific things that bother you about one another. The idea is to preempt such additions by being thorough. This will take time, and is the principal homework for the week. It's important. Be sure to do it, because much of what we will do in weeks to come may grow out of what's on these lists.

2. Be sure to "walk on eggs" this week. Stay out of fights and arguments. Rather than fight, write out any differences that you couldn't settle together and bring them in next time. If you forget and create problems for one

another, ask for and grant forgiveness and put it behind you. I recognize that you may not know all there is to know about biblical forgiveness, but we'll probably get into that in a later session. Any questions?

Sue: I don't think so.

Pastor: Bert?

Bert: Well, I'm not sure that I can come up with 100 items. Besides that, I doubt that I will have time to think about them.

Pastor: This is the first time you will have an opportunity to begin acting like a loving husband. Extend yourself, Bert, take the time, make the effort. In other words, give of yourself in order to begin to make this a marriage that sings. You can do it if you want to. Now, let's pray. [We don't simulate prayer. But we can say that Greg prayed that God would give them the encouragement necessary to have a productive week of working on their marriage.]

Let's pause to discuss...

Well, we've completed one session. Possibly in real time, it might have been more drawn out. But not much more so. Spontaneity in sessions is important. They should never drag. This one didn't. Of course, sometimes people will drag their feet, and it will be difficult to move at a normal pace. But try, nevertheless. Let your enthusiasm be catching. Help counselees to become zealous about doing fine deeds (Titus 2:14).

SESSION TWO

Bert and Sue arrived fifteen minutes late. "I wonder why," Greg thought. He was soon to find out. As they entered his study, he could see from the expressions on their faces that something was wrong, perhaps very wrong. They settled down in their chairs without much of a response to Greg's greeting and looked at their feet. Was this defeat, discouragement, despair – or what?

Pastor: It doesn't take a super counselor to see something's wrong. What happened?

[As Sue and Bert slowly lifted their heads their eyes met]. "Obviously," Greg thought, "each is hoping that the other will explain." [Finally, after what must have seemed an eternity to them, Bert spoke…]

Bert: Since I'm trying to be the responsible head of my home, I guess I should be the one to tell you. [Sue nodded.] I was fired. We're late because we were deciding whether to come.

Pastor: I'm really sorry to hear that, but in God's providence you can be sure that something good will come out of it. Tell me what happened?

Sue: He blew off steam at his boss yesterday, saying a few choice words, and the boss fired him. Disgusting, isn't it?

Bert: Do you want to hear the details?

Pastor: Perhaps later, but not now. Just let me say that no matter what your boss did or said, that was not a license for you to "lose it." He may have given you an *occasion* for your act, but he didn't *cause* you to do what you did. Your responsibility was to handle wrong doing rightly – supposing for argument's sake wrong was done. And "rightly" for a Christian means doing what God has told you to do in his Word.

Bert: I know, I know. I'm overwhelmed with guilt at what I did – just when we were beginning to work on our marriage.

We didn't need this thrown into the hopper. I guess this really messes things up.

Pastor: True, you shouldn't have done what you did, but on the other hand, as I said, by His providence, God may actually turn what happened for your good. In Romans 8:28 God promises that He works everything for the good of His children.

Bert: I just wish that were so, but I can't see that happening.

Pastor: Well perhaps, by God's grace, we can make it happen sooner rather than later. First, let me ask you, have you asked God to forgive you? And have you asked Sue as well? After all, she didn't "need" this either. [Bert indicates that he has and that he has received her forgiveness for the trouble he caused. Pastor Greg then continues...] Sue, you're awfully quiet. Where are you on all of this?

Sue: Bert expected me to blow my stack over what happened, but what good would it have done? One of us losing control is more than enough in any family. At first, I was furious inside, but then I remembered a verse in Proverbs I had just read that says, "A stubborn fool ventilates his anger, but the wise, holding it back, quiets it" (Proverbs 29:11). I did, and sure enough it quieted. I was able to handle it quietly – even *calmly*.

Bert: Actually, she was great! I couldn't believe how she reacted. If we could both do what she did all of the time, we'd have the "marriage that sings" that you've been talking about.

Pastor: You both can learn to govern your tempers. According to Galatians 5, self-control is one piece of the Spirit's fruit. This event has sobered the two of you, it seems, and made you think even more seriously about your marriage. If that's so, then in God's providence, He may have already begun to bring good out of evil! Let's take advantage of that and pick some of that fruit from His vine.

Sue: That all sounds good, but is it realistic? I mean since this happened, I wonder whether there is any hope for us? What do we do now?

Pastor: Certainly, it's realistic! Indeed, more realistic than our pitiful human responses to trouble. The Bible isn't pie in the sky, bye and bye, when you die; you can start slicing right now! There are three things you can do right away. First, we'll go on counseling as we intended to, giving you the time I promised. Second, we'll check up on your homework. Third, we'll decide what to do about Bert's job situation. Let's take up the second item now: your homework. Let me see your lists, please.

[Bert and Sue each hand over a page of items. Glancing at their lists, Greg makes the following comment.]

Greg: Well, Sue, it looks like you've put a lot of effort into making your list – you've got at least 150 items on it! And I notice, Bert has only supplemented it with five or six others. Taking a quick look at them – we'll spend time on them later – it appears that you've come up with a number of concrete entries. That's excellent. I expect them to be very useful. Now, Bert, I see that you list only 63 items, and the addendum that Sue placed at the bottom of your list has almost as many more. You made an effort, but it wasn't too strong. What kept you from completing the list?

Bert: Well, I was moving along working on it and actually getting somewhere when this thing happened. I lost heart. I thought that it wouldn't even be worth coming today. I was sure you'd throw us out for blowing it at work. So I gave up. Sue still wanted to do her part in spite of what happened, so she added those other items. It's only because *she* insisted that we're even here today.

Pastor: I see. Well, I can understand what you're saying, but losing your job is no reason for giving up. After all, you didn't *know* that I'd "throw you out," as you put it. Indeed, you guessed wrongly. If I were doing any throwing out, it would have been for not completing the list rather than for what happened at work. We need these lists as tools to help make the marriage what it should be in God's sight.[1] Granted, this complicates things a bit, but it's not a complete setback. We're certainly not going to quit counseling because you did what you did at work. That's when you need it most!

Bert: Well, pastor, I'm glad for that! I just didn't know. And you're right; I did act hastily.

Pastor: Okay. So much for that. We'll let Sue's additions stand as a part of your list.

Now, Sue, if we can postpone your account of your marriage difficulties until we have dealt with the job issue, perhaps that will be best. We don't want the matter of a job hanging over our heads, not dealt with. Right?

Sue: Right. As a matter of fact, even though it seems hopeless, I think the matter of the job should take precedence over all else at the moment.

Pastor: Okay, then. That's what we'll do.

Let's pause to discuss...

It's clear that what happened could have so disrupted things that counseling would have had to be curtailed, if not ended completely. But the pastor handled it well. And Sue's response was surprising. What made Sue act out of character? Normally, she would have been all over Bert. Instead, she turned to Scripture, applied it, and found help. Bert's right: as far as she's concerned, if their marriage could continue to go that smoothly, they'd soon have one that sings. Greg is thinking, "I wonder if Sue has gotten hope from our last session and is being careful not to rock the boat even before we put out very far into the stream." He continues thinking, "It could be that she never really wanted to divorce Bert. It may

---

1. Not returning to what it was before. Even at best, it seems that it would hardly have been pleasing to God.

all have been a 'crowbar,' designed to pry him lose from those things about him that disturb her. At any rate, given their past record, it seems that by comparison they handled a bad event exceedingly well. I must remember to tell them that, by doing so, they demonstrated that it is possible to do the same about other matters as well."

Bert seems genuinely conscience-stricken. On most other occasions, Greg might have lowered the boom on him for not completing his assignment. To his credit, Greg didn't, recognizing that matters were probably exactly as Bert described them. Nevertheless, wishing to make the point that undone homework in counseling is a serious matter, he did take the opportunity to stress the fact by his remarks on "throwing Bert out." That was a smooth reply on his part. At the same time, he deftly brought the issue to an end by allowing Sue's additions to complete Bert's list.

Sue has agreed to Greg's suggestion that they postpone her comments until after they deal with the job loss. They are wise in making this decision. After all, it would probably loom over whatever they talked about, no matter how they might try to dismiss it from their minds.

How will the pastor deal with the job loss? That's what we are just about to learn.

Let's continue…

Pastor: Okay, then. Let's get to the job problem. You're a civil engineer, aren't you, Bert?

Bert: Yeah.

Pastor: And you're telling me that you didn't act civilly toward your boss – right?

Bert: I guess you could put it that way.

Pastor: Perhaps in the future, you could take your job title to mean both what it ordinarily means, and also as a reminder of how you should always act at work. At any rate, tell me, generally, what happened. You can leave out any disparaging details about your boss. He isn't here, and we mustn't gossip about him. I'm mostly interested in what *you* thought and did.

Bert: Well, you see, I thought that I was next in line for a promotion at work. But when that stupid…

Pastor: Hold it! No name calling. Remember, it was your mouth that got you into trouble.

Bert: Okay. Okay. What happened was that instead of promoting me to a better position, he put someone, who was lower on the totem pole, in a position *over* me. That galled me to no end!

Pastor: No, it didn't "gall" you. You squirted all of that "gall" into your system yourself. What he did may have been all wrong, but so were you in responding as you did. You could have kept your cool. Since we're looking at Proverbs, consider this: "He who has a quick temper acts foolishly, but a man of discretion is patient" (Proverbs 14:17). It's patience and self-control that you lack, and we must work on those in days ahead. Well, I guess I have the bare facts – at least enough to know what happened to occasion your response. What did you say to him?

Bert: I called him "stupid," told him that his mother was a dog, and slammed the door as I walked out on him.

Pastor: I see. I appreciate the way you described your speech rather than quoting yourself exactly. Now, there are two things to do. One of them must be done right away. But first, let me ask what sort of work do you turn out? Are you good at it? Do you put in an honest day's work? Do you…

Sue [cuts in]: He's a hard worker. That's why I understand his reaction. He deserved that promotion. I know that doesn't excuse his behavior, but it surely explains it.

Pastor: Partially, at least. The other "part" is the sinful life patterns that he has developed over the years. That's why, when crossed, a person loses control. We'll have to deal with that matter in time. But for now, let me suggest that you call your boss first thing in the morning and ask for an appointment. If he's willing to grant it, you're one step along the path. Assuming that he does, you should go, hat in hand, admit your guilt, and ask him to give you the job back. After all, I suspect that it's hard to get civil engineers who are experienced in his company's policies and tasks – things that *you* already know. Tell him that you intend never again to do what you did, and ask him for forgiveness. If he agrees, thank him and ask if you could get to work right away. Don't let any grass grow under your feet.

Bert: Okay. It'll be hard, but I can do that. But what if he doesn't agree?

Pastor: That's when the second factor kicks in (but I hope that it won't be necessary to activate it). If he refuses to reinstate you, then you are to start job hunting *immediately*. Indeed, then you *will* have a job, after all. Your job will be to spend eight hours a day, five days a week, looking for a job. I can almost guarantee that if you do this faithfully – rather than moping around in self–pity all day, doing little or nothing, you'll find one fairly soon. You know the drill, don't you? Draw up a resume showing all there is about you and your previous employment that a prospective employer might want to know. But try to keep it brief and to the point. Call all of the headhunters to see what they have available. Talk to your friends about opportunities. And as a last resort, study the newspapers. But it's my hope and prayer that if you return to your boss, he'll take you back.

Bert: Okay. Okay. But what, exactly, should I say to him?

Pastor: Good question. What do *you* think you should say?

Bert: Well, I guess I should apologize and tell him I'm sorry I blew my stack when he promoted someone like John. How's that?

Pastor: Wrong in two particulars. First, you should ask for forgiveness, not apologize. Apologizing is the world's substitute for confession and asking for forgiveness, and it doesn't get the job done. Let me give you a little pamphlet our church offers about asking for forgiveness that will explain how it differs from apologizing, what's important to know about it, and how asking for forgiveness is a promise that you can keep whether you feel like it or not [Greg reaches for and then hands him a pamphlet from a rack on his study shelf].[1]

Now, there's one more thing. When you confess sin, be sure to talk only about yourself, not about other persons. Leave both your boss and John out of what you say. Remember, talk *only* about yourself. For instance, you might say, "I'm a Christian and I know what I did was sin. There was no excuse for my behavior. I want to ask you to forgive me, and if you can find it in your heart to do so, to reinstate me. But if you don't, I'll understand." Keep it brief, but don't leave out any of the details I've just mentioned. They're all important. Have you got it?

Bert: I think so.

Pastor: Then let me hear you say it. Pretend that I am your boss.

[Bert does, improving on his first attempt, but not well enough. Greg makes a few more suggestions, and Bert tries again. After two more attempts at fine tuning his plea, Bert gets it right.]

Pastor: Let's pray right now that you'll do well and that you'll handle whatever the outcome is as a Christian should. [All three take a turn at praying. Greg notices that Sue's prayer seems tender and earnest – a development that probably would not be true if she were holding strong animosity toward Bert.]

Pastor: Good. Now, Sue, let's hear what you have to say about the marriage.

---

1. For details on forgiveness, see my book *From Forgiven to Forgiving*.

Let's pause to discuss…

There is a good deal here to be noted. Greg's play on the words "civil engineer" was not an attempt at bad humor. This was no time for jokes, and he knew it. He meant it as a mnemonic device to help Bert think about being "civil" every time he heard, thought, spoke, or read those two words. His explanation – one that Bert accepts – makes that plain. Indeed, it seems that, should he follow it, the suggestion might turn out to be a real help to Bert.

It is obvious that throughout his counseling, Greg organizes things. People in trouble have a tendency to "roam all over the map." He keeps to one subject at a time, and works with it to a desired point. He may leave it for a time, only to come back to it again, but he alerts his counselees to that fact too. Such words as "first, second, next, later on, probably," pepper his speech. Notice how he warns Bert, *before* he relates the details of his encounter with his boss, not to speak "disparagingly" of him or anyone else. He focuses on Bert alone – on what *he* did and said. He takes the opportunity when doing so to explain that he can allow no gossip.

When Bert slips up, pastor Greg calls him on it. ("Hold it. No name calling.") And when Bert places the responsibility outside himself ("That galled me to no end!"), Greg doesn't let it pass. The passive, victim language that, as sinners, we have developed to excuse ourselves, must frequently be challenged – just as Greg does here. He rightly observes that the gall came from within. It's Bert who manufactured and delivered it. Greg also talks a bit from Proverbs about being slow to anger and speaks about the Spirit's fruit of self-control and patience. Probably in later sessions, at the appropriate time, he will be able to enlarge on the problem of anger and talk more about *learning* patience. Here, he merely sets the stage. Incidentally, you will notice how Greg keeps looking forward to what he expects to come next. That shows that he knows where he is going; and it helps his counselees to expect what is ahead. He keeps everyone looking forward. He wants them to expect good things to come.

Greg urges Bert to go confess sin, making it clear to his boss that what moved him to do so was his Christian faith. He gives detailed instruction about the elements that should be present in the confession.

While making no promises, he encourages Bert to think positively about the coming encounter and indicates that there is a possibility of becoming reinstated. But he also covers all bases: if Bert isn't called back to work, he will know exactly what to do next. Greg explains about the full-time "job" that would fall into his lap were that to be the case. He is preparing him for both alternatives.

The discussion about the job closes in prayer, and incidentally, Greg notices some tenderness in Sue's prayer for her husband. Tentatively, he interprets this as a good sign.

So far, Greg is endeavoring to help his counselees to understand something about the providence and grace of God at work in their lives. He uses this fact to encourage them, saying that this upset is not necessarily a set back. He could have elaborated on Romans 8:28–29, but evidently didn't think it necessary to do so, at least at the present time. Further instruction along this line may be needed in days to come. At this point, he doesn't want to bog the counseling down by too many mini-sermons.

Homework isn't fully taken into account, but he knows that he must examine – at least minimally – what they have presented even though the unexpected event at work has prohibited him from making a thorough evaluation and use of it in this session. He has stressed the importance of homework, so he treats it as such.

He gives Bert new homework about his future job status, but he hasn't given any homework to Sue. He must do so if for no other reason than to establish a set pattern of change at home following each session. Moreover, at some time he must give Sue the opportunity that he promised her to tell her side of their problems. So at this point, he asks her to do so.

Let's continue…

Sue: Well, I'm wondering whether I'm ready to go into our problems. I came last week loaded for bear, but now – well – things seem to have changed a bit, so I'm not sure of myself. I'll say a few words, but later, I may have more to say – if that's okay.

Pastor: Sounds fine to me. Go ahead, Sue.

Sue: Well, losing this job has done something to me. To tell you the truth, I discovered down underneath all of my anger something that I thought was gone forever. I actually felt sorry for Bert. Sure, at first, I was furious. But as I thought about the situation and read that verse in Proverbs, I calmed down and began to think deeply. I began to wonder whether I really want to divorce Bert. But don't get me wrong. That doesn't mean I've made up my mind.

When I came here, my mind was all but made up. If you hadn't offered some hope, I'd have gone back and gotten a lawyer. But now…? Well, since the problem occurred, I can't help thinking that Bert might need me. And…as hard as it is to say so…I might need him too. I hope that this isn't all sympathy that will wear off in a short time, rather than something deeper. I'm so confused…I'm not sure what to do.

Pastor: What you said seems to have come from your heart. Thanks for being so honest. Do you have to "do" anything at this point? What I mean is *anything such as you were thinking about doing*? Surely not. When confused, it is always unwise to make large decisions that you might regret later. The one thing that you can safely do is to continue to work at making your marriage a success. By "success" I mean making it a marriage that pleases God. What do you say?

Bert [breaking in]: Please say "Yes," Sue. I know now that's what I want more than anything else.

Sue: You do?

Bert: Absolutely. I never did want to split up, but it seemed inevitable. Now, all I want is to have the kind of marriage we've been discussing: one that "sings."

Sue: Well, that's interesting to hear. I thought you were on the verge of divorcing me!

Bert: At one point I was. But not now that I've come to my senses.

Pastor: I've been allowing you to talk to one another rather than to me because this is the kind of good talk that your marriage has been lacking. I think from what you're saying that there's only one thing to do: put your hearts and minds into making this marriage a "go." Am I reading you right?

Sue: Again, I've got to admit, I'm confused. Maybe it's all emotion that'll pass as soon as we start fighting again. I don't know.…I just don't know. But I guess there's no harm in trying. We can see where it goes. It's just that I hate to get my hopes up only to have them come crashing down around my feet in a couple of months. That would hurt!

Bert: Please, Sue.

Sue: Well, okay. But I'll be watching closely to be sure that what we do is the real thing.

Pastor: Exactly. That's what we want. Now, is there anything more that you want to say about the marriage, Sue? This is your time, you know.

Sue: I know that. But I'm not ready to open up completely right now. I asked if I could talk more later on, and you agreed. I think that would be best – when my head clears a bit – to do it then.

Pastor: Sure. We can wait. But meanwhile, we can begin to work on the data that we have. Since Bert has a difficult enough homework assignment for this week, seeing his former boss, we'll forego anything else on his part. But, Sue, we can begin to move ahead with you. Let's take a closer look at your list. [Greg picks it up and runs his eye down her entries]. I want to find a couple of items simple enough to begin with. Ah, here's a likely one.

Sue, you've written, "I often hit Bert with my troubles when he walks in the door from work. I ought to wait until he's had dinner and some rest before I tell him my woes." That's a great one. Since Bert's going to have a rough week of it seeing his boss, possibly having to look for another job, and the like, it would be great for you to work on this one. But if you fail, remember you can recoup by asking him for forgiveness. Read and reread that pamphlet on forgiveness. If you have any questions about it, bring them in next week in written form. Write them out so that you won't forget and so that you will remember exactly what the problem was. Do you think you can work on this?

Sue: Why not? It's easy enough. I just have to mean business.

Pastor: And let's be clear about one thing. Primarily, you are going to work at this because you want to be the kind of wife that pleases the Lord. You shouldn't do it out of sympathy or merely to please Bert. If that's your only reason, then you'll probably let up after the first disagreement you have with one another. But if you're doing it to please Jesus, that makes a great deal of difference. You've got no quarrel with Him!

Sue: I've got it.

Pastor: Good. Bring in a record of how well you did to the next session. Now, let's see…here's another one on your list: "I nag Bert about doing little things around the house – taking out the trash and so on."

Sue: Yeah. That's one of my principal faults.

Pastor: Okay. Which two items of this sort would you like to work on this week? I say "two" because I don't want to choke you by giving you too many to begin with.

Sue: Hmmmm. I guess the trash is one. I'll simply let it pile up and wait for him to see and do something about it.

Pastor: Good. Bert, you can help Sue. Start by noticing the trash and doing something about it on your own.

Bert: Will do.

Sue: I think the second thing is his socks. He throws them on the floor at night and I have to put them in the hamper the next morning.

Bert: I'll work on that too. If I forget, please remind me gently – not nag me. Okay? I really want to develop better habits about both of these matters.

Pastor: I've written a note about each item while you've been talking to help remind you of your commitments. Here it is. Sue, I suggest that you copy one for Bert when you get home.

Sue: Thanks. I'll do it.

Pastor: We could talk longer, but it seems to me that we've accomplished a great deal today, and you both have a trying week ahead of you, so let's call it quits for this session. I'll be waiting to hear good things from you at the next one. Now, let's pray. [Greg does, asking for God's blessing and help for them over the next week.]

Let's pause to discuss...

What a session! There was *remarkable* movement by both Bert and Sue. A crisis can often bring matters to a head. Is that happening here? True, there are no final commitments, but they are working together somewhat, beginning to do things for one another and talking *civilly*. Any idea what the next session will be like? It is hard to predict. If Bert loses his job for good, that may have all sorts of consequences. If he can't land another right away, fear about finances may set in and that could occasion serious quarrels. It's better not to speculate – better just to pray.

Greg finally got Sue to talk a little, and to agree to some initial homework. She didn't have much to say about the matters she had in mind when she came to the first session, but what she did say was revealing. There seems to be some doubt about it, but it's just possible that she wants the marriage to last. She is cautious, somewhat confused by her own reactions, and uncertain about making any large commitments. As she said, she doesn't want to get hurt if it all falls apart. But she is seeing some daylight over the horizon. When she first came, all was pitch-black darkness! Getting some hope is what has brought about the change that has occurred.

Greg is hoping that there will be no setbacks this week. He wonders how they will handle the events that, in God's providence, will unfold. He muses, "It would have been helpful if I could have spent more time discussing providence, but you can't do everything in every session. They *are* reading their Bibles it seems (at least Sue is), and it's clear from what God has already done by her use of Proverbs that He may continue to use Scripture for His purposes quite apart from what I may or may not say and do. So I guess I can safely leave them to learn that way as well as from my exposition and application of it." Greg must check out Bert, however – is he or is he not regularly reading Scripture?

Is this seemingly remarkable progress going to continue? What might Greg do in the next session to see that it does? How can he capitalize on and solidify the gains already made? These are the sorts of matters he is thinking about in anticipation of the third session. You might do so too.

Session Three

Bert and Sue arrive early this week while the pastor is in his study still counseling someone else. When he says, "Goodbye" to the former counselee, Bert rushes in.

Bert: Pastor, I got my job back! Thank you so much for helping me know what to do and say. If you hadn't helped, I probably would have made a mess of things. Thanks again!

[Both Sue and Bert seem happy, and that portends a good session Greg decides.]

Pastor: Great! Glad to hear it. Have a seat and we'll talk about it.

Sue: He went with fear and trembling, but it turned out that things weren't so bad after all. His boss expected him to come back, and said he hoped that this experience had taught him a lesson.

Bert: And it has! I've learned that I've got to get my temper under control.

Pastor: You're right. And you know why, don't you?

Bert: So I won't lose my job for good!

Pastor: Yes, but that's not the main reason. Above all else, you must do so in order to please God.

Bert: Yes…of course…you're right. And because I didn't answer your question right, I guess that means that I still have a lot to learn about being the right kind of Christian…And, the right kind of Christian husband too.

Pastor: Good. Now it seems that you're even beginning to *think* like a Christian should. So let's get down to work. How'd your homework go?

Sue: Just a minute, pastor. Tell him what else your boss said.

Bert: Oh, sure. I forgot for a minute. He told me to ask you to send a report on how well I'm doing after a month or so. Would you mind doing that?

Pastor: That's interesting. I suppose you told him you were coming for counseling.

Bert: Yes, I did. And he thought that was super. Can you do that for me?

Pastor: Did he make that a condition for taking you back?

Bert: No. But he said he thought it would be good to do so. He has a son who gets into trouble all the time because he won't keep his mouth shut. He may want to send him to you.

Pastor; I'd be glad to talk to the boy. And sure, I can send his father a report. But remember because I am going to be honest about what I tell him, you'd better shape up quickly!

Sue: Right. That ought to keep Bert on the stick.

Pastor: Yes. And as I hope you can you see, in God's providence, various aspects of this problem are beginning to work themselves out. Is the boss or his son a believer?

Bert; My boss? No. I met his son once, but there was no indication one way or the other. I suppose, too, that there's been little in me to indicate it one way or another either.

Pastor: This may be your opportunity to become a vital witness for Christ to the whole family. You want to be sure that you don't fail. Before we get into your homework, let's ask God to bless you, your boss, and his family – especially his son. [All three pray.]

Pastor: Now, how about the homework?

Sue: Well, for one thing, I was supposed to avoid hitting Bert with problems when he walks in the door from work.

Pastor: How'd she do, Bert?

Bert: Great! What a difference it made!

Sue: He didn't mention the one day I messed up.

Pastor: Oh? Tell me about it.

Bert [breaking in]: Given the other four days, it meant nothing. I'm not even sure why she's mentioning it.

Pastor: You may mean well by covering it up. But understand, the more I know, the more I can help. Sue, thanks for not minimizing things. Sketch for me what happened.

Sue: Sure. It was one of those days – cat went up the curtains. Tried, that is. But curtains came down. Pot of stuff I was cooking boiled over while I was on the phone trying to get rid of a troublesome neighbor. And…well, I'm sure you get the picture. On top of all of this, kids got into a fight. Not an argument, but a real pier #9 fight! Tommy socked Billy square in the eye as hard as he could hit him. And I went ballistic. I had hardly calmed down when Bert came walking through the door in such a good mood. So I guess I was jealous of how well his day must have been in contrast to how rough mine was, so I hit *him* in the eye with all my troubles – verbally!

Bert: And she knows how to sock a guy when she wants to!

Pastor: After goofing up, what did you do about it? That's the important thing to discuss at the moment.

Bert: I ducked. That's what I always do when things like this happen.

Pastor: What does that mean?

Sue: It means that he went into the other room and pulled the paper down over his face!

Bert: Yeah. Instead of dealing with the problem as a thoughtful husband, I reverted.

Pastor: Looks like you abdicated your authority for doing good as a husband!

Bert: Yeah. Some headship!

Pastor: But it gives us a good opportunity to discuss your response. What could you have done differently that would please God?

Bert: I thought about that the same night. And since Sue got some help from reading Proverbs, I decided to do the same. So I flipped through it to see if I could get any help. Sure enough, right there in the 15th chapter, I ran into a verse that said, "A soft answer turns away wrath." I knew then what I should have done.

Pastor: What was that?

Bert: I should have allowed Sue to calm down, and then, in a kindly, quiet way asked her if there was anything I could do to help her.

Sue: If he had, I'd have asked him to talk to the boys and – as the "head of the home" – to deal with their shenanigans. Instead, he did nothing.

Pastor: Sounds sensible. Bert, it also sounds like you learned something from *this*.

Bert: Sure did.

Sue: So did I.

Pastor: What did you learn, Sue?

Sue: To work on cooling it the way that I did when he lost his job. Instead, I yelled at the kids and tore into Bert. Neither one of those responses was necessary. And they were both hurtful.

Pastor: And displeasing to God. Do you remember what the Proverbs passage you quoted last time said about "cooling it"?

Sue: Yeah. It said to "hold it back." I suppose that means I should wait long enough to get control of myself before reacting.

Pastor: Right. And It's important to learn *how* to "hold it back" don't you think?

Sue: I was wondering about that. How *do* you do it?

Pastor: Another verse from Proverbs should help. It goes this way: "The ear of the righteous considers how to answer, but the mouth of the wicked pours forth evil things" (Proverbs 15:28). That's in the same chapter Bert was looking at. The word "consider" has in it the idea of "studying." If you pause long enough to consider or study a matter – what your answer should be like and what effects it will have – not only will your anger begin to abate, but you may also even think of something helpful to say. In other words, you want to *take time to think before you answer.* Taking that time, "holding back" in order *to think,* will make all of the difference.

Sue: Sorta' like counting ten, eh?

Pastor: Sorta'. Counting ten is one way of holding back one's temper. "Considering" and "studying" what to do and say is a better one.

Bert: I can learn from that too. It would have been a lot better if that's what I'd have done instead of spouting off before my boss.

Sue: I agree. And I see how that applies to my response to the kids and how I spoke to Bert. Wow! Isn't Proverbs a wonderful book?

Pastor: It certainly is! Since you've discovered it anew, I suggest that you read together one chapter a day each month from Proverbs. It's almost designed, it would seem, for that kind of reading since there are 31 chapters – just about a month's reading.

Bert: Great! As the head of the home, I can do that every night after supper.

Sue: And after reading, we can talk about it and pray.

Pastor: Couldn't have come up with better suggestions myself! Now, Bert, what about your homework?

Let's pause to discuss…

Well, things don't usually go this well. Looks like Greg's got an easy one this time! Both Bert and Sue not only respond well, but seem to be catching on. Of course, it has taken some guiding from Greg, even when they do. For instance, it is probably because Greg has been insisting that pleasing God is basic to all else that Bert realized that he not only needed to become a better Christian, but "the right kind of Christian husband too." It's interesting that the boss asked for a report. Is Bert's supposition correct? Is his boss thinking of putting Bert on probation? Or is he up to something else?

Why did Bert try to cover up for Sue? Was it out of mistaken kindness, or was he trying to get some "brownie points" from her? It's good, however, to see that Sue did well 4/5 of the week. That was an improvement. But the "jealousy," as she called it, came from contrasting her day with Bert's. That's not right, but Greg seems to have missed telling her so, at least at this point. He could have emphasized how destructive jealousy is. And he might have worked on it a bit.[1]

Was the altercation between Tommy and Billy typical of boy-sinners, or is it indicative of a greater problem? Greg may have to delve into that in time.

It was good to hear that Bert went to Proverbs for help. And Greg again took advantage of this to quote another verse that showed Sue (and Bert) how to hold back anger and to urge them to read Proverbs together regularly. Bert and Sue seemed to take hold of the suggestion and run with it. That is probably an indication that they're growing. Let's hope that it continues and that the enthusiasm doesn't peter out in a short while. If Sue comes around, Bert may want to relax rather than take advantage of the situation to further his marriage.

---

1. To do so, he might have read and applied James 3:16.

44

Greg can't help asking himself, "Where is the hostility that I had discerned in the first session? Is it gone? Is it dormant, waiting to see if each partner continues in his or her resolutions before God?" He concludes, "Bert clearly seems to want to keep the marriage intact. But I'm not sure about Sue."

Taking hold of what he learned about Bert's boss and son, it was helpful for Greg to suggest praying for them. Moreover, Greg expressed interest in Bert's Christian witness. He stressed the need to be careful about this for their sake, and Sue suggested that shaping up will also keep Bert "on the stick." That means he is out on a limb not only at home before Sue, but also before the boss. And – preeminently – before God.

Look at all that happened through homework! So much teaching and learning can be accomplished when counselees do their homework. They will learn better, sooner, and also in more practical ways. New problems and opportunities emerge from homework. Corrections in attitudes and actions also are easier to come by. And if you asked him, it's almost certain that Greg would put in a plug for homework – as would every successful nouthetic counselor. Think what they all would have missed if he hadn't given Sue that assignment!

Let's continue…

Bert: I got the socks in the hamper six out of seven times, forgot on Saturday!

Pastor: Something like Sue, you both made a pretty good attempt.

Sue: Well, I know you might not think that it's very much of a thing for him to do, but I want to tell you it was just such a good feeling not to see them on the floor!

Pastor: I'm sure it was. You know, Bert, great changes in attitudes can result from small changes in behavior. It showed – concretely – that you were making an effort to do something to please Sue. Now, be sure you don't let up. And let's work on seven out of seven, just as Sue is working on five out of five! Now, for the other assignment. It was a kind of double whammy: it involved you taking out the trash and Sue not nagging you.

Sue: I didn't nag him, and I didn't get any results either!

Pastor: Are you telling me that he didn't take out the trash?

Sue: That's exactly what I'm telling you. As a matter of fact, it's still sitting there smelling up the entire house.

Pastor: And he hasn't noticed?

Sue: Not so far as I can see.

Pastor: You're awfully quiet, Bert.

Bert: What can I say? She's right. I didn't notice it. I never do. In fact I even forgot the assignment altogether.

Pastor: Did you post the homework assignment paper I gave you?

Bert: No.

Pastor: I suggest that you dig it out and put it up in a place that's conspicuous to you.

Bert: You're probably right. I'll need a reminder. So much is happening these days since we came here that I hardly know whether I'm coming or going.

Sue: Excuses, excuses!

Bert: Not really – explanations.

Pastor: The assignments weren't all that arduous. You could have done them all this week. Were you getting cocky about what you did achieve and thought that this wasn't necessary?

Bert: Maybe so. I'm not sure. But this coming week – the trash leaves the house when it should! I guarantee that!

Pastor: Sue, let me ask you, Did you fret about the trash? I hear that you didn't nag him about it. How did you handle it?

Sue: Well, I kept thinking, "He'll wake up and take it out today."

Pastor: But when he didn't and the week went by, what were you thinking?

Sue: Two things: "He doesn't really care enough about me to do this one simple thing." And, "I'll be darned if I'm going to tell him about it; he can go to counseling and face the music."

Bert: It's not that I don't care, it's just…

Sue: If he really cared, then he'd have done it.

Pastor: May I make a suggestion? Since he did do pretty well with the socks, it seems he must have cared some. Perhaps he's stuck more deeply in this trash pattern than he thinks. [You'd almost expect Greg at this point to say, "Trash the pattern" wouldn't you?] We'll see what happens this coming week. But regardless, Bert, notice what happened. I asked about the trash, and Sue answered in terms about you caring. Did you get that? You see, just as I said when discussing the socks, large changes in attitudes can take place over small changes in behavior. Can you see now what I meant by that?

Bert: Yes, I certainly can.

Sue: Well, we'll give him another week to prove he cares – and then a week after that, and one after that, and so on.

Pastor: You won't nag him about it?

Sue: I won't. But he'd better do as he's promised!

Pastor: Or what?

Sue: Uh…I'm not sure. But for starters, you'll hear from me about it!

Pastor: Okay. Better for me to hear from you than Bert. Now tell me about the week in general. How are things going? And what are you thinking about your marriage at this point?

Bert: I'm clear on one thing: I don't want to get a divorce and I don't want her to get one either.

Pastor: Why? Because things are going better?

Bert: Yes, that's for sure. But even more so, I've been thinking about that Dobson article and about what the marriage counselor advised. I think that they were both unbiblical. I had a long talk with one of the men I work with who is a Christian and he convinced me from Scripture that there was no basis for us to get a divorce. As you like to put it: I want to please God in this. I'm convinced that what we have to do is to work on our marriage to make it one that God wants it to be.

Pastor: Now, those are a couple of interesting conclusions that you've come to. How do they grab you, Sue?

Sue: Well, this is the first time I've heard him talk that way. I haven't had time to think them over.

Bert: I mean it. I really do want to become God's kind of husband.

Pastor: Sue, do you have any convictions about whether a divorce would be right or wrong before God? Are there still those lingering doubts that you expressed two weeks ago?

Sue: I don't know. There's the issue of incompatibility for one thing. If we're really incompatible, how can we ever make it?

Pastor: Of course you two are incompatible. There's no question about that. In fact, all sinners are incompatible! They're born that way. They want what they want and others can go hang. Love, as we looked at it in a former session, is the answer. People can become compatible only when God gives them love and enables them to become compatible. That's one thing that Christianity is all about: becoming compatible with God and with one another. It is something that you learn by the grace of God.

Sue: Well, I never thought of it that way. Hmmmmm. I think I'll want to hear more about that. But for now, you obviously think like Bert that a divorce would be wrong. How come?

Pastor: I try to think like God, not like Bert! Well, a divorce is allowed for believers only on two grounds – adultery and desertion, neither of which, so far as I know, is true in your case. [A pause; no response, so he goes on.] Even then, it's not mandated, only permitted. And there is no basis for not trying to put a marriage that's on the rocks back together again – in ways that are new and better – because that pleases God. Christians can always make it – if they really want to and do what God requires. What do you think of that, Sue?

Sue: You're the pastor, and should know better than I. But a man like Dobson – how could he be wrong? He says that a wife under certain circumstances – if her husband feels suffocated – can open his cage and let him go.

Bert: I'm no bird! And I don't want to fly away.

Pastor: I know it's difficult for laymen (or should I say "laypersons"?) when Christian leaders differ. But it's the responsibility of every Christian to determine what the Bible says on matters like divorce. We can't depend only on others. I'm going to lend you a book that explains the biblical truths about divorce. It's entitled *Marriage, Divorce and Remarriage in the Bible*. Your homework this week, Sue, is to read it through and write out any questions that you still have after doing so. And, Bert, don't bug her about it, just let her read it without trying to find out what she's thinking. We'll find that out next week. Will you read it, Sue?

Sue: I guess so. It doesn't look too fat. I think I can digest it in a week.

Pastor: Start reading right away. The book may be slim, but it will challenge you to do some real study of your Bible. It may take you longer than you think.

Now, Bert, let's consider some homework for you. For starters, remember the trash. That's a repeat assignment. Don't let up on the socks. How about working on this one on you list: "I have a hard time being mushy. I suppose I should

49

tell Sue I love her more often." We dealt with the mushy nonsense earlier. Remember what love is – basically?

Bert: Giving what another needs.

Pastor: Right. Now how can you express your love for Sue?

Bert: By giving her something she needs?

Pastor: Right. This week, you are to think of at least five things Sue needs that you could give her. Keep away from flowers and that sort of thing. Study Sue and determine some real needs. These should be things that don't cost much – preferably things you don't even have to buy. Bring in your list, and determine an order of priority as to what you should begin giving and then so on through the list. Got it?

Bert: I think so.

Pastor: Here, I'll write it out for you. [He does and hands the assignment slip to Bert.] Don't forget to post it. Now, I think that we have reached a breaking point. Let's pray and I'll see you next week. [They do.]

Let's pause to discuss...

It was good also to see how Sue handled the trash incident. Though she seemed rather upset about it, the prospect of going to counseling helped her to keep her cool. She seemed a bit too tense about the matter, but she has learned something about holding back her anger and cooling it. Incidentally, Greg might have told her that one of the Old Testament words for anger is, literally, "to be hot." So the modern expression "cool it" that she used seems quite appropriate as its opposite. Another key Old Testament term for anger is "to snort." There's no need to explain that, is there? As you hear the counselees tell about how well they did their homework, it seems that both made a genuine attempt. And as I said earlier, the pastor did as every counselor should do, he picked up on what was or wasn't done and moved into other areas as a result of what he learned. The socks gave him an opportunity to show Bert that picking them up was interpreted by Sue as concern for her. And that not taking care of the trash was interpreted as the opposite. Bert learned through this that concrete efforts truly do make a difference in attitudes.

In answer to Greg's request to talk about the week in general, Bert firmly comes out in the open about his desires for the marriage. He has rejected the idea of a divorce for two reasons. He wants to continue the marriage, and he has come to believe that it would be wrong biblically for them to divorce. A Christian friend has helped in this regard. This gives Greg an opportunity to explain that there are only two legitimate reasons for believers to divorce, and that then, there is still no absolute necessity to do so – God can always pull the marriages of genuine believers out of the fire. Greg doesn't go into the refinements of the matter such as the place of church discipline, for instance, but since Sue is still dubious, he hands her a book to read for her homework. It would have been nice for the church to provide such books as free handouts, so that Greg wouldn't have to "lend" books. That's something for him to work on.

Notice how deftly he handles the psychologist's view of incompatibility. He turned that right around – as indeed the facts require him to. What he said seems to have stunned Sue. It probably took away one of her principal arguments for thinking of a divorce. That the pastor gave her a book to read rather than to try to do all of the exegetical and theological work involved in understanding divorce biblically in the session was wise. It seems that for his age, Greg, who is now only 46, has gained a lot of wisdom. And he dealt with the difference between his view and Dobson's rather smoothly. He didn't waste time getting into a fight about that. He let the book do his arguing of the case.

Emphasizing the fact he taught them earlier that loving is giving, Greg was able to stress that point by assigning Bert the task of coming up with five loving things to do for Sue. He doesn't actually say to do them, but to make a list based on his observation of Sue's needs. If he does that, it will begin to get him thinking about Sue in ways that he hasn't in the past. And of course, it will provide some material and work for future counseling as well. Things are still going well. Will they continue that way? This is only the third session. Too early to tell? Probably. Greg is beginning to think about his estimate of six to eight weeks and wonders if it will take that many. But he doesn't say so.

SESSION FOUR

As this session begins, Greg thinks that he notices a certain coldness on Sue's part. Because he cannot be sure, he makes no comment about it as they take their seats. But it seems that he is right from the way that Bert keeps on glancing at her as if he were expecting something untoward to happen. The pastor speaks.

Pastor: Well, it's good to see the two of you again. How did your homework go? Socks and trash up to snuff, Bert?

Bert: Yep.

Pastor: Good. How about the homecoming each night?

Bert: She did just fine.

Pastor: Have you got the list of things that you can do for Sue – ways of giving of yourself?

Sue: Before we get into that I have something to say.

Pastor: Yes?

Sue: You know that book on divorce you gave me? Well, it's no good.

Pastor: What did you find wrong with it?

Sue: I didn't bother to read it.

Pastor: You didn't? How come?

Sue: It was written by a kook! Why should I waste my time?

Pastor: A kook? How did you come to that conclusion?

Sue: Well, the guy who wrote it is well-known as having no scholarship behind him, and practically every Christian psychologist thinks he's wrong.

Pastor: Where did you get that idea?

Sue: My friend who gave me the Dobson article told me all about him. And she's the leader of a women's Berean Bible Study Group.

Pastor: I'm afraid your friend is mistaken. Yes, he does oppose eclectic counseling – mixing pagan ideas with biblical truth. But not scholarly? He studied at three seminaries, majored in Greek at Johns Hopkins University, earned a Ph.D. at the University of Missouri, completed a post-doctoral course with a former head of the APA at the University of Illinois where he worked in two mental institutions, taught doctoral students as a professor in two seminaries, founded a counseling institute, is a member of the Academy of the National Association of Nouthetic Counselors who certified him, translated the entire New Testament and portions of the Old, published a set of commentaries on the New Testament, has spoken in countries all over the world, and has authored over 100 books. Evidently, your friend has picked up some false gossip. Some of those who oppose his views on counseling have been known at times (intentionally or unintentionally) to spread errors about him.

Bert: Well, I told Sue she ought to investigate for herself, but she persisted in believing what her friend said.

Sue: I'm impressed with the credentials you've just spelled out, but I just don't know.

Pastor: You won't know until you take the time to study the question of divorce from a Scriptural perspective. We all need to know what God says about it – not what Dobson or some other non-theologian has to say. Those who oppose the author of that book, for the most part, have no seminary training, don't know Greek or Hebrew, have shallow theology, and have spent their lives studying what worldly psychologists have to say rather than what the Scriptures teach. The book I gave you is an exegetical study of biblical teaching about divorce. I suggest that you read it after all.

Sue [grudgingly]: I guess I'll have to. But I'll read with a critical eye.

Pastor: Good. Wouldn't have it any other way. Be sure, however, you give the book a fair chance. Your friend may be trying to help, but I wonder how well versed in the Scriptures she really is. Some women's study groups are an opportunity to meet and pool ignorance as they fill in white space in booklets that ask questions but provide no answers. Because she handed you that Dobson article which advised the opposite of what God says in the Bible, it makes me think that she needs to read the book herself. It's not wise to take counsel from two persons at the same time. It's like holding a candle in your hand and lighting both ends: in time you'll get burned.

Sue: We'll see.

Pastor: You'll read it – agreed?

Sue: Yes.

Pastor: Now, Bert, what did you come up with by way of "giving" of yourself to Sue? Let me hear your list, and please, don't tell me you forgot to do it!

Let's pause to discuss…

Sue is torn between her friend and her pastor. While Greg doesn't argue the case against divorce with her – the time may come when he will have to do so – he does indicate that she has received some bad counsel from her friend. Greg more than adequately (he may have gone overboard here) demonstrates by the list of the author's credentials that Sue's friend is badly misinformed. He questions the validity of some women's study groups that she may be a part of. By doing so, he hopes to counter her serious misrepresentations. And he makes the important point that it isn't wise to take counsel from more than one source at a time. Few things confuse counselees more than doing this. It is sad to have to deal with unnecessary problems of the sort that so often arise when one does so.

Bert's new homework is about to be assessed. So far, both he and Sue have been keeping up on their old homework assignments. If they continue to do so, over a period of six weeks or so, they may acquire new patterns that will last. That's one thing Greg is looking forward to.

This is the fourth week of counseling. It has run into a snag. It is debatable whether or not Sue will read the book. Will she opt for her friend's advice or her pastor's? Will she talk to her again and be led farther astray? These are some of the questions that are running through Greg's mind. While the problem may not be too serious, it could be devastating. But God can work such things out remarkably well, as we have already seen in previous sessions.

Where should Greg steer counseling next? Perhaps something will grow out of Bert's homework. Let's see.

Let's continue...

Bert: No. I didn't forget. But I could only come up with four items.

Pastor: How much time and thought did you put into it?

Bert: A good bit more than you'd think with the little I have to offer you. I just keep drawing a blank every time I sit down to think about it.

Pastor: Obviously, your old patterns of thinking of self rather than what you can do for others – especially Sue – are hard to break. But by God's help, you can change them. Indeed, this very assignment, carried out to the full, may be exactly what will help you begin to do it. One way to turn your thinking around is to do what I Peter 3:7 says: "Live with your wives in an understanding way." You understand so little about Sue's needs because you haven't been doing that.

Bert: Probably you're right. But what does the verse mean?

Pastor: At least this: take time to study her so as to understand her better. Understand what her wants, her desires, and her longings are. But to begin with, you can understand some of the practical things that she needs day by day.

Bert: Okay. I get it. Watch her, observe day by day instead of going on in my merry old way, not giving a second thought to such things.

Pastor: Right.

Bert: But I did come up with four things. Do you want to see my list?

Pastor: Yes. [Bert hands it over to him.] Hmmmm. This is an interesting list:

1. Fix broken vacuum cleaner handle.
2. Spend time with the kids on Saturday so Sue can be freed up.
3. Clear the table after meals.
4. Take Sue out for dinner once a month while having a baby sitter stay with the boys.

As a matter of fact, what you've listed are all good items. Don't you agree, Sue?

Sue: Can't argue with that! The only question that I have is will he do them, and if so, for how long?

Pastor: Bert, are you listing them in order of priority?

Bert: I don't know which should come first. Any ideas, Pastor?

Pastor: Frankly, I suspect that #2 on your list would be the most helpful at this point. What do you say, Sue?

Sue: If he'd do it, that would be great! But – I have my doubts.

Pastor: You sure do have doubts about all sorts of things – don't you, Sue? In I Corinthians 13:7, Paul talks about "believing all things and hoping all things" as a characteristic of love. If you want to show love to Bert, then give him a chance to prove he means business. Why discourage him with your doubts?

Since we happen to be discussing doubt, do you know what James says about doubting? Listen to this comment about those who ask God for something but doubt: "That person shouldn't suppose that he will receive anything from the Lord" (James 1:7). In that passage he also describes the plight of the doubter: "a person who doubts is like a wave of the sea that is driven and tossed by the wind" (verse 6). Then he goes on to say that this is "because a double-minded man is unstable in all of his ways." I know that you don't want to be like that and miss the Lord's blessing in your life, do you?

Sue: If I didn't know that you mean well, I'd say you're insulting. How dare you compare me to such a person?

Pastor: The last thing I want to do is to insult you. I'm trying to help you. But this is what *God* says about doubters, not me. And it seems that in some respects at least, it does apply to you. You seem tossed about like a wave of the sea when it comes to whether or not you want the marriage to continue. You are blown about by counseling on the one hand, and on the other hand, by your equally windy friend. What am I to think? It doesn't seem too far out to make that application. Honestly, now don't you believe that there's something to it?

Sue: Humph!

Pastor: What's that mean?

Sue: It means that I've had it. I'm leaving right now, and I don't know whether I'll be back next week or not! [Sue gets up and heads for the door, which she slams as she leaves. Bert stays seated.]

Bert: Pastor, I'm sorry for this. I'll go home right now and in a kindly way try to assume the headship that I thought I had but have been lacking. One way or another, at least you'll see me next week. Keep the appointment open.

Pastor: See you then, Bert. And, I suggest that you work on item #2 on your list.

[Bert leaves, catching up with Sue.]

Let's pause to discuss…

Oooh! What's happened now? Has Greg done the unthinkable: telling Sue the truth, truth she'd rather not hear? Was he too abrupt? Could he have waited to say this? Is she cheesed because he showed up her friend as a mere gossip? Because he suggested her Bible study might be froth? She came in looking and acting cold. But is that anything new? She's been toying from the beginning with Bert and the Pastor – up one time and down the next. She refuses to come down hard on a number of things – the really important ones. She has done her homework up until the book incident. So, does that mean she's trying? Or is she just biding her time to see if Bert will shape up? Has Greg stepped on her pride? Why else would she react this way? She should have taken what he had to say seriously enough to go home and evaluate her life. So far, her course in counseling has been a series of indecisions. Greg is likely to be right: she's a "wave." If she is indecisive about one thing, according to James, she will be so in "all" her ways. And as we have seen, this seems to be a trait of hers. What is to be done now? Pray. And don't back down.

Bert's final comments were interesting. Bert has been profiting from counseling – learning and attempting to apply what he learns. He doesn't seem to be so swift at catching on as Sue, but he seems more willing to do what God wishes. Will they both be at the church services on Sunday? If so, that may be an indication that she has settled down a bit. Will she come next Monday with Bert? We can only wait and see. It would be wrong to run after her. That may be just what she wants. And, it might seem that Greg was backing down on the Scriptures he quoted. Of course, he should admit it if he makes a mistake, does wrong, or fails in some way, but he doesn't think he has. So he must stand fast.

We all await next week – unless something happens before then.…

SESSION FIVE

True to his word, Bert showed up on time for counseling. Greg could see nothing of Sue as he entered so he thought, "Well, we've probably lost her." Settling down in their chairs...

Greg says: I suppose Sue decided she's had enough of counseling, right?

Bert: Oh no. You don't understand. She's not here because we had to come in two separate cars. She was out shopping, and...well, you know women – when they go shopping they often lose track of time. I'm sure she'll be here soon.

[He had no more spoken those words when in through the front door of the church and down the hall toward the study strode a bedraggled, puffing, red-faced Sue.]

Sue: Sorry to be late, the shopping and the traffic were terrible! Whew! I'm bushed!

Pastor: That's okay. Sit down and pull yourself together for a moment. You look exhausted. We haven't started yet. You're only a few minutes late anyway. Glad to see you back.

Sue [after a minute of gaining her composure]: I'm okay now. I guess I'm glad to be back too. First thing – I want to ask you to forgive me for my uncalled for behavior at the last session. I was wrong, I know it, and I never want to act like that again. And wouldn't you know, it was just when I thought that I was doing so well at holding my temper about other things. Think of that! I guess I just got ticked off by your suggestion that I am as changeable and uncertain as a wave of the sea. I seem to have certain buttons that if you push I take off like a rocket. But, who knows? You may be right – uncertainty and doubt may be at the heart of my problems. At any rate, please forgive me.

Pastor: Certainly, I'll forgive you. That's what repentance and forgiveness are all about. Fundamentally, repentance is changing your mind to see things God's way, and then acting in accordance with it – a change of mind leading to a change of action.

Sue: But I did read the pamphlet on forgiveness and I think that I understand what just took place when you forgave me. You are promising that you're not going to bring it up and use it against me any more. I guess I have a lot more to learn.

Pastor: We all have a lot to learn! Yes, it seems that you learned a key point from the pamphlet. Keep it on hand for the next time you may be involved in a forgiveness transaction – either asking for it or granting it.

When I saw you in church yesterday, I was encouraged to think that you might decide to return for counseling. I didn't get to talk to you then, and that's just as well because it's best not to mention counseling matters in public. Someone might overhear just enough to get a wrong idea.

Bert: Or a right one!

Pastor: Well, that too. Sue, tell me how things are now.

Sue: When I left here, I was angry enough to chew nails! But then I remembered all of those verses in Proverbs and my resolution to learn to control my temper. So I prayed about it and settled down. Then, I asked myself, "What am I going to do now?" And there was only one answer I could give: start reading the book to give it a fair chance. By the way, I've kept doing all of my other assignments too. And I sure did appreciate Bert taking the kids on Saturday! Now, that's what I call a good assignment, and good homework on his part!

Pastor: It sure is. So now that you've read the book, what do you think?

Sue: I only intended to read a few pages to see if the author really is a kook. But as soon as I got into it, I found that it was hard to put down. I read the whole thing. It made me get my Bible out and follow along. And what it said really did seem to make sense. If nothing else, I concluded that he's no kook.

Pastor: I knew you would. The book is a serious biblical study of the question. Have you come to any conclusion about the matter of divorce?

Sue: No. But I'm leaning away from the Dobson view. Tell me one thing. You said that we're all incompatible. I want to be sure to get that straight. How did you mean that?

Pastor: What I meant was simply this: we're all born sinners. And as such, we want our own way, just as Adam and Eve did in the garden, and just as everyone else since does (except Jesus). Well, our "way" isn't God's way (as He tells us in Isaiah 55:8). Our way is to do what we want in order to please ourselves rather than to do what God wants in order to please Him. As a result, our sinful ways make us incompatible with God. That's why Jesus had to die for us: otherwise, we'd all be outcasts of His Father's heavenly home forever. Apart from Christ, we're too incompatible to live with Him in heaven! He alone makes it possible to obey the first great commandment – to love God with all our heart, mind, body, soul, and strength (Mark 12:30). And since the second great commandment is to love our neighbor as ourselves, and we can't fulfill any of God's commandments apart from salvation,[1] we are incompatible with one another as well.

Sue: We sure are a sorry lot, aren't we?

Pastor: Apart from Jesus Christ.

Bert: I know now that my wanting to divorce Sue was because I wanted my own way. I simply didn't want to love her as *myself*. At heart, I've been nothing but a self-centered lout! My goal now is to be the kind of husband who is a loving head of his home.

Sue: But, Bert, aren't you being a little hard on yourself? Talking that way seems to fly in the face of the favorable self-

---

1. Cf. Romans 5:5, where Paul says that true, biblical love enters only when the Spirit is poured into our hearts.

image and right self-esteem that you ought to have, doesn't it?

Bert: I don't know, but in spite of that, it's just how I'm thinking at last.

Pastor: May I say something about self-image, self-esteem, and self-love?

Bert and Sue [respectively]: Yeah, please do. [and] Go ahead. It should be interesting.

Pastor: Actually, there's no place in the Bible that says we ought to have high self-esteem. It wasn't until Abraham Maslow, an unbelieving psychologist, popularized this thinking about self that anyone ever dreamed of promoting it. The first extant sermon preached in the colonies was entitled, "The Danger of Self-love." Until the present generation, the words "self-love" always indicated a self-centered attitude that was to be avoided and condemned. In Scripture, we are never told to love ourselves or to strive for a high self-image. Indeed, Paul thought that people have the opposite problem. He wrote that we are "not to think more highly of ourselves than we ought to" (Romans 12:3). This emphasis on self-centeredness has led to a "Me-First" generation.

Sue: I never heard that before. I understand that Dobson, for instance, says that having self-esteem is what everyone needs to solve his problems. And I've heard Christians say that the command to love one's self also means we ought to love ourselves too. Isn't that a biblical reason for self-love?

Pastor: I know people talk that way, but think carefully. In Matthew 22:37–40 Jesus spoke of only two commandments, not three. He said "on these *two* commandments hang all the Law and the Prophets." Those who use the passage to teach three commandments distort the plain meaning of the text in an attempt to support their views. Because we already love ourselves a great deal, Jesus was saying that we ought to have at least as much love for others as we already have for ourselves. Does that help?

Bert. It does. I never did think that this self-esteem, self-love emphasis was Christian.

Sue: Hmmmmm. I'll need to turn that one over in my mind for a while. It does seem to make sense. After all, everybody knows that self-centeredness is to be avoided. Is there really that much difference between that and self-love? It doesn't seem so, but…well, so many people teach otherwise.

Pastor: Would you like another book to read about the matter by the same "kook"?

Sue: Don't tell me…

Pastor: Yes, he did write on the subject. Here, if you want to borrow it, I have a second copy available.

Sue: Okay, I'll take it. I think I'd be interested in what he has to say about this question. By the way, here's the book you loaned me. [Sue reaches into her purse, pulls it out, and places it on Greg's desk.] Do you know where I can get a copy for myself?

Pastor: Sure, we carry it right here at a discount in our church bookstore. See Mildred [the church secretary] before you leave and she'll take care of you. Well, we've been into so many things, and it's already the fourth-and-one-half session. I think it's time to start taking stock. After all, we can't go on counseling forever.

Let's pause to discuss…

Whew! It looked bad for a while. But in her slow – almost grudging way – Sue seems as if she might be coming around. Yet given her track record, it would be wise to hold back judgment on that matter. Doubtless, Greg is breathing a sigh of relief. But we must hope that he doesn't assume too much, try to move too fast, and so on.

He does recognize that there has been a lot dumped on the table in these five weeks, and it appears that when he says "let's take stock," he is going to sum up what has happened, determine what has been accomplished, and decide what needs to be done next. If he doesn't do so, he may leave all sorts of loose ends dangling that should be tied up.

One thing he has not yet been able to do is give Sue the opportunity to give her account of the marriage difficulties. Perhaps she never will. It may be she really doesn't want to any more. Or perhaps she is afraid to open old wounds, now that there seems to be some progress.

And with Bert, there has been steady growth. In the face of seemingly serious set-backs, he has kept his composure, he has done his homework, and he has been growing in his understanding and convictions. He has locked on to the idea of becoming a loving husband, and there seems to be genuine hope that he will pull it off.

Sue is still her uncommitted self, uncertain about most things, but it seems that, in spite of herself, she is slowly making progress in the right direction. When Greg contradicts Dobson in this session – not overtly, but by teaching the opposite from what he teaches about self-esteem – she raises no objection. It's possible that the "kook's" book on divorce has convinced her that Dobson isn't a trustworthy expositor of Scripture. Or at least it may have given her serious doubts about the validity of what Dobson's article advocated. That is, perhaps, a sign of progress. And when he does in order to expose the flawed teaching in many women's Bible studies, she takes it in stride. In addition, her willingness to receive another of the "kook's" books seems to portend progress as well.

Bert has been working hard to bring her to some kind of commitment, throwing out lines for her to grab hold of, but she isn't grasping them and he isn't pushing. Should he begin to do so? Or should he wait until he is sure of being on firmer ground? Will he ever be sure of anything about Sue until her doubts and uncertainties begin to disappear? Pushing her to say something definitive could be pushing one of the "buttons" she mentioned. If so, Greg will have to deal with that. But on the other hand, should he let that "button" scenario simply slip by. Why not? Did he miss it? Did he think that they were handling enough at the moment and let it pass, or did he possibly shelve it for later appraisal? Only Greg knows. But it seems that he's sharp enough not to simply *miss* it altogether.

Homework seems to be going well. Sue was deeply impressed by Bert's relieving her of the children on Saturday. You could hear it in her words. Indeed, was it this that brought her back? Or perhaps, was it a combination of that and the fact that the book she read so caught her attention that she realized she needed to learn more? It's interesting that she is willing to reconsider her ideas about self-esteem and seems to be anxious to read the book on the subject that her pastor offered her. This, if nothing more, will probably keep her "on the string" until Greg can help her solidify her beliefs.

We would like to hear more about what happened when Bert went home with her after she walked out of counseling. The conversation in the car, as well as those conversations that took place during the ensuing week, might be valuable to explore. Do you think that Greg will do so? If he does, will he ask Sue or Bert to open up the subject? Bert said he'd like to handle matters as a loving husband should. Did he? Asking that might launch him into the matter. What did Bert do and say? How did Sue respond?

Let's continue…

Bert: No, we can't. But how many more weeks do you think we will be coming here for counseling?

Pastor: At this point, that's unpredictable. It all depends on the progress we make. I guarantee you that I won't keep you any longer than I think necessary. But sometimes people want to leave too soon – before they've solidified their gains.

Sue: That makes sense. We've spent this much time here and in doing things at home that we don't want it all to go to waste.

Pastor: Exactly. And speaking of what you are doing at home, let me ask you a question or two. When you two abruptly left here in the middle of the last session, what happened next? Bert, you told me as you were leaving that you wanted to handle the upset as a loving Christian husband should. How did that work out?

Bert: Well, there was virtually nothing said in the car on the way home. I figured I'd let Sue cool off before I addressed the matter. By the time we'd arrived home – as you know we drive about twenty minutes from our home in Stone Ridge to church – it appeared that we would still not be in shape to discuss anything. So, I simply said, "Sue, as your husband, if there's anything I could say or do to help you in this matter, I'd like to know what it is." And she answered, "I'll let you know when I'm ready to talk." Normally, I'd have told her off for answering abruptly, and there would have been a fight. But Proverbs has helped me too, I suppose.

Pastor: Did she?

Sue: I certainly did. Eventually. I told him two things – that I felt insulted, but that I am sorry for what I did.

Pastor: What happened then?

Sue: He hugged me and asked, "What are you going to do about it?" and also, "Can I help?"

Bert: She said, "Not now. But thanks for asking." Then she told me that she was going to pray and read more in Proverbs. That sounded good to me, so I encouraged her. I offered to pray with her, but she said she'd prefer to pray alone. So I left her to her reading and prayer.

Pastor: Well, Sue, what happened next?

Sue: I did just what Bert said. And he Lord used Proverbs again to bring me up short. As I read, Proverbs 12:16 struck me squarely in the face. You know, pastor, how it says, "A stupid fool's irritation is known immediately, but the prudent man ignores an insult." Nothing could have been more direct and applicable than that! I lacked "prudence." I guess, among other things, that means good judgment. And worse still, I had acted as a fool! So I asked the Lord to forgive me, reread the pamphlet on forgiveness, and determined right then and there to come back to counseling. Over the next few days, as I thought about what had happened, I also concluded that what I had considered an insult, really hadn't been intended that way at all. James was the one who talked about the wave and the wind – it wasn't your idea. You were probably trying to help me recognize my indecisiveness. That's all. And while I might agree or disagree with you about that, I realized that what you said wasn't intended as an insult at all.

Pastor: It sounds like you've done some serious thinking. Let me commend you on it. Now, let me hazard a question: Have you thought about the matter of doubt and uncertainty any more?

Sue: I thought you'd bring that up. Yes, but I'm uncertain (there goes that word again!) about it. I guess I am somewhat of an "uncertain" person. But I don't think it's because of doubt about God's promises. I think it's uncertainty about myself.

Pastor: I'm glad to hear that you're willing to plant your feet firmly on Scripture. Clearly, you've shown that over and over again as you read, accepted, and did what God said in Proverbs. Now, since that's true, let me remind you of that verse in Philippians 2:13: "…it is God Who is producing in you both the willingness and the ability to do the things that please Him." If that was happening to the Philippians, it can also happen to you. You need not be uncertain of yourself when it is God Whose task it is to produce good things in you. You once said that it's hard to have your hopes dashed – that it hurts. I know that. But when you trust God, He never fails you. Hopes are realized! We saw that in I Corinthians 10:13 where He promises to be faithful to His Word. If you ask God to help you with your uncertainty and to give you courage to step out onto His promises in faith, He'll do it. He'll produce in you the very same willingness and ability to do what pleases Him as He did for the Philippians.

Sue: I'll think about that and try to take it to heart. It's possible that behind my uncertainty – and I can see that I really am uncertain about many things – maybe a basic fear of being let down. So I may be holding back – afraid to wholly commit myself to the marriage. I'm wavering... Oh! There I've virtually called myself a "wave." But I am wavering about the matter of getting a divorce. It doesn't seem like there are grounds for it, and there seems to be some hope that we could put the marriage back together again. So, I'm going to keep on working at it to see what happens. Bert has surely changed – for the good. Maybe I can too!

Bert: Thanks, Hun. I appreciate the fact that you've noticed my efforts. And let me tell you, whether you realize it or not, you've begun to change too. With Pastor Greg's help, I'm sure we can pull it off!

Sue: I hope so. We'll see if it lasts.

Pastor: You can pull it off. And if you mean business, it *will* last. Now, I think that this may be a good stopping place for today. We still need to take stock a bit, but that can wait till next time. Right now, it's time for...

Sue and Bert [in unison]: Homework.

Pastor: You've got it! Bert, let's begin with you. On your list of four items, number one was to fix the handle on the vacuum cleaner. Will that be difficult for you to do?

Bert: Not at all. The only problem I'll have is going out to get the part and taking time to do the work. But before you say it, I know this is an opportunity for me to show love toward Sue by giving of my time and effort to fix it. I'll do it. Even though it'll mean hurrying over to the parts store after work before they close.

Pastor: Good. Now, Sue, let's look at your list. I see that you've mentioned "failure to serve meals that please Bert." What do you mean by that?

Sue: Well, I know what he likes to eat. And it isn't always the sorts of food that I like. So, I guess I've selfishly brought and cooked the things that I wanted to eat over the years, forgetting his preferences altogether. I suppose you'd say that I was self-centered and incompatible in acting that way.

Pastor: What do *you* say?

Sue: I guess it's true.

Pastor: Then this week, why not make at least two meals that focus solely on Bert's preferences?

Sue: I'll do it!

Pastor: Good. Before you leave, Sue, listen to yourself talk. I think you'll discover that there's one word that you say over and over again. Now let's pray.

Let's pause to discuss…

So Greg did pick up on some of the things that we were wondering about. He looked for an opening to talk about what happened after the incident when Sue walked out, and he found the opening. He learned a lot about both Sue and Bert from what they did after the altercation. Bert was very tactful and showed love. Sue became thoughtful, and went to God's Word again. Once more, Greg used it, and it had a powerful effect on her. And did you notice, she wants to continue counseling because she doesn't want to waste what has been accomplished? That's significant. She recognizes that there has been progress.

Sue handles herself well in this session. She even pokes fun at herself when using the word "wavering." But her fundamental, foot-dragging, lack of commitment is still there. It must be changed! Do you know what is the one word Sue frequently uses? Why do you think he sent her away wondering what it was? Greg hazarded a question. Why did he use that word? Because it was about the very issue that Sue had handled so badly – her uncertainties and doubts. Greg carefully prepared the discussion by assuring Sue that he had noticed her willingness to accept Scripture and act on it. Then, he urged her to trust God to help her with her lack of trust in herself. He mentioned her fear of being hurt again and that God could enable her not to fail, but to be willing and able to do the things that please Him. Should Greg have gone out on a limb about this matter? Yes. Why? Because unless he gets to the heart of this matter, he will continue to experience Sue's holding back. If any real, lasting progress is to be made, Sue must commit herself to restoring their marriage. He recognizes this, and seems not to want to spend more sessions dancing around the problem. Will he press her on this during the next session?

Session Six

From the smiles on their faces and the jovial attitudes that they seemed to have, Greg figured that Bert and Sue had a good week. After exchanging a few pleasantries, everyone sat down and Greg began.

Pastor: Well, here we are at what is usually about a mid-point or better in counseling. As I said last week, it's probably time to take stock and discover where we are in the process that we began five sessions ago. But before we do, let me ask you, how was your week?

Bert: In many ways, the best yet. And to boot, I had some of those good meals I like.

Pastor: Sue?

Sue: I agree.

Pastor: Wonderful! You have decided, then, to stay married. Right?

Bert: Definitely.

Sue: I'm leaning that way.

Pastor: Sue, your response reminds me of something: I left you with a conundrum last time. Remember? I asked you to figure out what word it is that you use so frequently that it seems to characterize your approach to counseling – perhaps even to life. Do you know what it is?

Sue: No. To tell you the truth, that one baffled me. I guess I just don't listen carefully enough to what I say!

Pastor: Well, you just used it again in that last sentence.

Sue: I did? Well, I guess that…

Bert: That's it! The word we were searching for all week was "guess." Right, pastor?

Pastor: Bert, you got it!

Bert: You even used it again in the sentence that you were about to speak before I chimed in. By the way – sorry for that!

Sue: Hmmmmm. I guess I do use the word often. Oh, I just said it again!

Pastor: What do you think might be behind the overuse of that word, Sue?

Sue: Well, I gu... I *think* that it might represent my basic uncertainty about things concerning our marriage.

Pastor: I think you're right! It seems to me that by now you ought to have decided that you are going to put all you have into making yours a marriage that honors God – one that is a good example to your children and to others in the church who also may be having problems. Are you convinced yet that you have no biblical grounds for getting a divorce? You can't keep this matter up in the air forever. What do you think, Sue?'

Sue: I think so, but even if saving the marriage is the right thing to do, I'm not sure that it will turn out as it should. Now, you just mentioned the children. I think if I could get some satisfaction about them it might go a long way toward making up my mind. And I want you to know that I'm *not* changing the subject.

Pastor: What do you mean?

Sue: Since we've been having a hard time of it, we've been so preoccupied with ourselves that we've kinda' let the children go. I suppose that shows a lack of love for them – putting ourselves first. But nevertheless, it's true. We've lost the control of them that we once had; I'd say that they have become very undisciplined. And all of this turmoil has made it difficult to think about the future. Divorce might seriously hurt the children, but so might continuing on as we have. Can you help us out of this dilemma?

Pastor: Certainly. And I'd be delighted to help you work out a program for disciplining them. We can take the first steps here tonight.

Bert: Good. As a loving head of my home, I want to be sure that I care for them as I should – including giving them proper discipline.

Sue: You've never done much disciplining Bert – I've had it all on my shoulders. You know that. Don't make it sound like you have!

Bert: Now, Sue, you know how hard I've tried, but to be honest, you also know that you always contradict what I tell them and they get confused. In time, I finally gave up. I now know that was wrong. Here, pastor, is one of the areas in which I need to learn headship.

Sue: Humph! [with some bitterness in her voice] All I ever did was fill in when you abdicated your position. As if you'd ever really *tried* to – you…

Pastor: Whoa! Hold it! I see that I'll have to enforce the rule we established early on: talk to me, not to each other. I relaxed it because you were doing so well. Now, Sue, what were you about to say?

Sue [calmer now]: I was about to say that Bert leaves all of the discipline to me. Then, when something happens, I get all of the blame.

Pastor: Do you see it that way, Bert?

Bert: Only partially. Sure, she ends up doing all of the discipline because she won't let me do it. I've tried and tried, but every time I do, she interposes her own ideas and the kids don't know who to follow. And as a result, they learn how to manipulate us. They use one of us against the other. So I guess you might say, trying to be a "giving" husband and father, I back off.

Pastor: Now, wait a minute. That isn't being a "giving" husband or father at all. Giving isn't giving *in*. Giving isn't giving *up*. It seems that you've been doing both.

Bert: Well, yes. You might say that. But what can I do when she insists on having her way?

Pastor: I'm going to help you learn how to solve the problem of discipline – and many other problems as well – by a way that should be very helpful if you follow it closely. Are you willing to hear it?

Bert: I'm all ears.

Sue: Sounds like magic again. But I'm listening.

Let's pause to discuss…

Wow! Greg's really struck oil it seems. And that promise – what in the world is he going to propose? Here is an area of conflict that has not surfaced before. It seems that it's the cause of a lot of tension in the marriage. Sue may not be wholly telling her side of the marriage difficulties, but she's lighted on one item that is obviously a source of serious concern to her and contention in the home. Notice, she grabbed on a thread dangling from Greg's comment and pulled the subject loose. Now that she's unraveling it, Greg is entering into an important part of their lives. If he can pull this one off well, it seems Sue will be more willing to work on their marriage. What they have accomplished so far has gone a long way toward calming things down at home – except, it seems, for this matter. Here, Greg has reached a crucial point in counseling. Perhaps lack of discipline is *the* major issue between them. A breakthrough here is what we need.

It seems that the focus on the word "guess" hasn't gone anywhere. Did it just fall flat or did Greg allow Sue to deflect that discussion by bringing up the children? If so, did he do so intentionally, or did Sue take over control of the counseling at that point? She says that she isn't trying to change the subject. Does she mean that this matter is fundamental to her indecisiveness? Does she see her family out of control? Is she so concerned about the future of her children that she has considered divorcing Bert in order to "save" them from a bickering, quarrelling home? There is probably much here that will come out if the matter is handled well. Doubtless, Greg sees this as an opportunity not to be lost. He dives in rather than going back to "taking stock," which he's tried twice but hasn't yet been able to do. Perhaps taking stock isn't so important at this time anyway. One thing that you see Greg doing throughout is steering a course *flexibly* toward the ends he has in view. As new material comes into sight, he evaluates its relative importance and decides whether or not to go with it. He is willing to keep changing his immediate agendas if it seems wise to do so. But one thing: Greg was stressing the issue of whether or not Sue's proposed divorce is scriptural – and left it. Was that a good thing to do? At this point, is it more important to go with the child discipline matter? Another judgment call!

So let's see what Greg has to propose to Sue and Bert.

Let's continue…

Pastor: No, it isn't magic. It's better than that – as I said before. It's better because magic only pretends; this is for real. But the success of what I'm about to describe will depend entirely upon you two as you pursue it before the Lord, asking Him for wisdom and strength. I am proposing that you set up a conference table in your home. Now let me explain what that is and how it works. Okay?

Bert: Sounds interesting.

Sue: Have at it!

Pastor: Here's what I have in mind. I propose that you both sit down for half an hour three times a week to confer about matters such as child discipline. Let's begin with that issue. Here is how it works: Bert – as the head of the home – is responsible for calling the conference at an agreed-upon time and place. After sitting down, Bert reads a portion of the

Scriptures. Then Sue prays that God will give them wisdom, clarity, and patience as they discuss matters.

There is to be no arguing, fighting, name-calling, or anything else that might disrupt true biblical decorum. You are to act as Christians at the table. In the unlikely event that either one of you violates that rule, the other silently stands. He or she will simply wait there until the other says, *nicely*, "Okay, please be seated and we'll continue." The two of you will then begin to confer again. Now, there should be no argument about whether the other person should or should not have stood. Just leave it to his or her discretion – whether you think it was called for or not – and begin conferring again.

Sue is to act as secretary. In your conference book (purchased and used for conference notes), in addition to the conference date, she is to record three things:

1. What is the matter under discussion.
2. Whether an outcome satisfactory to each is reached.
3. If not, reasons why:
   a. More time is needed to complete the discussion
   b. The parties involved couldn't agree
   c. Some other factor, namely _____
      [item mentioned]

The conference should be closed with prayer by both participants.

If there are unresolved difficulties, continue to pray for a resolution and meet in conference again to see if any new light can be shed on the problem. In discussions, be sure to give biblical reasons for points of view. If the outcome is the same, bring your notes to the next counseling session.

Now, I suggest that this week you begin your conference sessions with a consideration of the problems connected with child discipline that you are experiencing. Take up only one specific problem at each session. Begin with the easiest to settle, and having done so, then – and only then – move to the next, and so on. I'll give you the first week's topics as a freebee. At the first conference session, together compile a list of ways the children are getting out of hand. You'll need that to work on problems. At the second session, record ways you know that the Lord would have you do a better job of disciplining your children. Record all the thoughts that come to mind, and list biblical references (as best you can) for each idea. At the third session, reevaluate what you have recorded, shape up the list, agree on as many of the items listed as you can, and bring it to counseling at the next session, together with any items you disagree about. Is that clear?

Bert: It's a lot to remember.

Pastor: Yes, but I'm going to hand you an explanatory guide for the conference table that will keep you on track. Everything I've said is there, plus some examples of what these things look like. And I have also written down what to do at the three conference sessions this week. Are you ready to do it?

Sue: Yes. If this will lead to peace in the home, it's worth trying.

Pastor: Remember, that's a lesser goal. Above all else, you should do this to please God. Secondarily, do it for the children's sake, and then for the peace that it brings you. May I suggest that you read Ephesians 6:1–3 and Hebrews 12:5–11 at your conferences this week? I'll write those references down for you. And remember, there is a host of verses on child-rearing in your favorite book – Proverbs. I suggest that you check them out!

Now, let's get back to the matter of divorce. Sue, am I right in thinking that you now believe that there is no biblical reason for divorce?

Sue: I gue…Yes, I've come to think so after reading the book you gave me.

Pastor: Good. Now, that means the matter is settled without any question, and you are committed to making your marriage what a Christian marriage ought to be. Right?

Sue: I'd like to believe that's possible, but I have no evidence that it will happen.

Pastor: Should you wait for evidence or move ahead by faith?

Sue: I know the answer you want, but I have little faith in myself or in Bert.

Pastor: It isn't faith in yourselves that I'm talking about. It's faith in God and His promises in the Bible that counts. Faith in God and His Word is better than evidence. Remember Hebrews 11:1: "Now faith is a solidly grounded certainty about what we hope for..." You see, to trust God is to believe in a "certainty!" Can you see that?

Sue: Yes, I understand what you're saying, but I don't want to get hurt!

Pastor: The writer of Hebrews goes on to say: "without faith it is impossible to please Him [God]" (v. 6). And in that verse, he continues, saying, that when believers do trust Him, he "rewards" them. He expects them to seek His help. You see, it's not a matter of you and Bert doing this alone. You can "seek" God's help and you can be sure that He will help you when you determine to obey Him.

Sue: I do believe God and His Word. You saw how following what God said in Proverbs helped me. But "faith"? Now, that's another matter. I doubt that I have enough faith to endure all it'll take.

Pastor: When they asked for more faith in order to do something difficult, Jesus once told His disciples that it wasn't a matter of how *much* faith they had – it was a matter of obedience. This passage in Luke 17:5 and 6 is one that you need to consider. Fundamentally, committing yourself to doing what God wants you to do to restore this marriage is a matter of *obedience*, not a matter of how much faith you have. Jesus told them, "if you have faith like a mustard seed" you can do wonders! So if you have any faith at all – and you do as we have already seen – God can do wonders for your marriage through you and Bert. How about it, Sue? Are you ready to commit yourself to obeying God in this matter – by faith?

Sue: Well, I've tried everything else, but I never tried faith.

Pastor: Isn't it about time you put the matter into God's hands and follow His commands by faith?

Sue: If I don't, I know that I'll displease God. So…I gue… No! I *will* do it. But I'll need God's help.

Bert: Thank the Lord!

Pastor: Wonderful! Every command of God is a reason for hope. You see, He commands nothing that He will not provide the wisdom and strength to do – if you "seek" it from Him. Are there any questions before we pray?

[Hearing none, Greg prays, hands them the Conference Table Guide, the references mentioned, and their assignment for the three conferences, and says goodbye.]

Let's pause to discuss…

Well. Greg did have something concrete in mind – the conference table. And if they take advantage of it, doing as they are supposed to, his counselees will find help. And, as he says, "That's not magic!" Once again, Greg has to make it clear that whatever is done, above all, must be done to please God, not primarily to gain relief. Bert seems to have caught on to this biblical emphasis. If Sue and Bert read carefully, they will see that Hebrews 12:11 says that it is righteousness that produces peace as its fruit. Righteousness, as it is used in this passage, refers to righteous living before God. Could Greg have worked out this point more fully?

The matter of Sue's indecisiveness is out on the table for inspection. Finally, Greg is able to dig into it. He is convinced that, basically, she wants to save the marriage, but is still hesitant to commit herself for fear counseling will turn out badly, probably because of Bert (though at this juncture he has given her little reason to think that way). So Greg goes for broke,

81

showing if their marriage is to succeed, it will do so out of God's blessing obedient faith. And it seems, he gets a commitment! Divorce is no longer an option for her, and Sue knows it.

The discussion of faith is crucial. After all, in the final analysis, the uncertainty and doubt that Sue expresses is a matter of faith. So Greg has worked the discussion around to where he began. Remember how Sue became angry at James' statement that a person who doubts will receive nothing from the Lord, and that in prayer he must come in faith to God? Now, rather than seeing this as an insult, Sue is contemplating the matter of faith as the means to a better marriage – one that honors God.

Greg has said that by this session that counseling should be at or near a mid-point. He is preparing his counselees for the fact that it will come to an end, perhaps sooner than they realize. If they think that they can take all the time in the world to get all the necessary things done, this ought to make them think twice. But at the same time, he is careful not to make any predictions. There is much to be done so they must go to work doing what God requires. Did mentioning the fact that counseling must end, and suggesting that it might do so in a few weeks, push counseling forward – at least to some extent? If so, was that good or bad? Would they hurry along omitting significant matters, or would they work harder at bringing counseling to a proper conclusion? Either could happen, so Greg must watch carefully to determine which may be occurring. Things have been going fairly slowly. In one way or another, it is time now to move more quickly. If there has been a genuine breakthrough, then they will.[1]

---

1. Concerning the importance of the breakthrough session, see my book, *Critical Stages of Biblical Counseling.*

SESSION SEVEN

Greg could tell nothing from the demeanor of his counselees as they entered the office. He always looked carefully for a clue as to how they might respond to counseling. By doing so, he could usually set the tone of the session to match their moods. But, as such measurement is inexact, he is not always correct, as we have seen at the outset of other sessions. So tonight, having no clue, he began the session.

Pastor: I'm looking forward to this session as a vital one. Not that some sessions are unimportant, but given the progress we've made thus far, this one could be the turning point. How did it go this week? [Not knowing how else to set the tone, Greg notes the vital nature of what might happen at this juncture.]

Bert: Good and bad, but mostly good.

Sue: Bad and good, but mostly bad!

Pastor: Well, it seems that you both agree on one thing – there was good and bad. Tell me about it.

Bert: Go ahead, Sue. You've been anxious to tell pastor Greg what happened.

Sue: Okay. Let's start with the good. We had our first conference table and came up with sixteen rules for the children. I think that was pretty good.

Pastor: Actually, that was the "bad!"

Bert: What? We worked hard on those rules, and without even looking at them, you say our efforts were bad? How can you say that? Do you mean to say that we didn't do anything good then?

Pastor: Do you want to become a warden watching every move of your little prisoners?

Bert: Of course not. But what are you getting at?

Pastor: If you set up sixteen rules, you'll be doing nothing but watching to see if they are obeyed. Sixteen is far too many. The children won't be able to remember them, and if in the unlikely event that *you* will, you'll find that there are too many to enforce. But if you fail to do so – and you can count on that – then you will teach them that when you set up a rule you don't really mean business. Better to lay out two rules at a time and strictly enforce them.

Sue: Ah! Now I get it! That does seem to make sense. But I guess we did a lot of work for nothing.

Pastor: No. Over a period of time you may want to institute all of them. But never set up a new rule until the children have learned to obey former ones. It's that simple.

Sue: You say two is enough for the time being? Which two would you like us to work on for now?

Pastor: Why don't *you* tell *me* which two you'd like to begin enforcing? After all, soon you will have to make such decisions on your own without my help, so why not begin now?

Bert: All right. How about this for one: *direct disobedience?* By that I mean we should have a rule about when they defy our authority by refusing to do as we direct, say "No," or words to that effect.

Pastor: Excellent! That's the basic rule that backs up all the rest. What do you think of Bert's choice, Sue?

Sue: I agree that it's a good first one. But I'm also interested in which of the remaining fifteen Bert thinks we should establish.

Bert: Well, subject to your approval, Sue, I was thinking of number six.

Pastor: Which one is that?

Bert: That the kids help Sue by picking up all of their toys and putting them away in the toy box every night before supper.

Sue: Bert! You really came through with that one! There's nothing that annoys me more after a hard day than having to yell at them to do so or, in frustration, having to pick them up myself. I concur!

Pastor: Good choice, Bert. That was acting like the head of your house. You put Sue first. So we now know something of the homework that you will begin with this week.

Now, let's consider some other aspects of rule-keeping that you need to know or you may fail in your endeavor. First, always attach the penalties for breaking a rule ahead of time. Let the children know exactly what they will be, and never vary in carrying them out. Always be sure to choose penalties beforehand, in calm circumstances, or you will be issuing penalties on the spot that you will regret imposing later on. Penalties, not carefully thought through, are usually bad penalties. Also, always be sure that the penalty fits the crime.

Second, if, for instance, you say that certain toys will be put on a shelf for the rest of the day, that doesn't allow you to shout, scold, or show frustration. Putting up with that sort of thing isn't part of the penalty, anyway. Remember that, work on it, and you will find yourself less harried by infractions.

Now, we also must settle on punishments for the two rules that you have chosen. For the first – "direct disobedience," as you rightly called it – nothing less than spanking is appropriate. Do you agree? A spanking should hurt, but not injure.

Bert and Sue [respectively]: Absolutely. [and] Yes, by all means.

Pastor: Okay, then, how about the second rule?

Sue: I suggest that if the toys aren't picked up one day, then they should all be confiscated and locked up on the next day.

Pastor: What do you think of that penalty, Bert?

Bert: Well, I have some misgivings about it. For instance, if there are no toys to play with the next day, they will not know what to do with themselves and they'll drive Sue nuts!

Pastor: In other words, we might ask, "Who is it that's being punished?"

Sue: Good observation, men! Hmmmm. What punishment should we agree on then?

Pastor: I suggest that for a part of this week's homework you think about and agree on a proper penalty. Remember, the punishment should fit the crime: not be more severe or less so. For a while, the kids will forget and break rules, but don't give them any slack when they do. Otherwise, you'll fail to train them. When they learn, they won't forget any longer.

Now, there's one more thing. After a spanking, there should be a time of "reproof." Listen to this verse from your favorite book: "The rod and reproof impart wisdom, but a youth allowed to be on his own disgraces his mother" (Proverbs 29:15). And parallel to that verse, God says in Ephesians 6:4 that we must bring up children with "the Lord's discipline and counsel." That means that our training must involve not only corporal "discipline" (the "rod"), but also "counsel" ("reproof"). Following the spanking you should always take time to talk about why this was wrong and why you must spank them. And when they seek forgiveness, be sure to hug them!

Sue: That makes all kinds of sense. I suppose that when talking to them, we should explain that they must obey their parents as Ephesians 6:1 says they should. That's a verse that they have been learning to recite in Sunday School.

Pastor: Yes. But you should also tell them that they should obey you because God gave them to you to look after and train so that they will become the sort of boys that God wants them to be. Put the emphasis on God's ultimate authority, and yours as derived from Him. When they fail, you should make it clear that they are sinners who need God to help them obey. Tell them that's why Jesus came, and take the opportunity to explain the Gospel to them.

Sue: Now, all of this sounds like things we needed to know and that, if we do them faithfully, will make a great difference in the home. Why didn't somebody tell us this before?

Now, let me tell you the bad news – how we failed this week. We had a heated disagreement about whether I should discipline children on the spot or whether we should wait till Bert comes home and let him discipline. He thinks on the spot; I think later. What do you think?

Pastor: Of course, what I think is unimportant. But let me read a couple of verses to you that tell you what *God* thinks. Then, *you* can tell *me* what you ought to do. First, Ecclesiastes 8:11, "Where a sentence on evil is not speedily executed the result is that the hearts within the sons of men are entirely intent on doing evil." And Proverbs 13:24 says, "He who holds back his rod hates his son, but the one who loves him chastens him right away." Now, what's the answer?

Sue [reluctantly]: I suppose Bert's right. But…

Pastor: Do you "suppose," or are you *sure* he's right? If so, there should be no "buts."

Sue: Okay. He's right. My hesitation and indecision was coming out again!

Pastor: Now, there will be times out in public (in the grocery store and so on) when it would be inappropriate to spank a child instantly. The thing to do is to quickly withdraw to a quiet, private place and take care of the matter. Otherwise, you will find that people who have no business getting involved, will – in one way or another – try to intervene.

Sue: Good. I was wondering about that. Now let me continue with the bad news. When we couldn't agree about several things, I got mad and walked out.

Pastor: You know the rules for the conference table. I don't need to repeat them. Obviously, that was one way of ignoring them. But what I'm most concerned about is how the two of you handled matters when that happened. Tell me about it.

Bert: I stood up a couple of times – to no avail. So I sat down and started reasoning – again, to no avail. Then, she walked out.

Pastor: Did she get up to walk away before or after you began to "lecture" her?

Bert: After. And I guess you're right – it was a kind of lecture.

Pastor: What do you think would have happened if you had obeyed the rule not to talk, but just stand?

Bert: I'm not sure.

Pastor: Sue, what would have happened?

Let's pause to discuss…

What do you think Sue would have done if Bert had obeyed the rule? Would they have been able to work their problem out? Bert has insight into matters of discipline, it seems, when he points out why it wouldn't be wise to take away all the toys from the children for a whole day. On this, Sue seems to need help to think things through.

Bert also is in line with the Scriptures on the immediacy of punishment. But is this merely because he doesn't want everything to fall on his head when he comes home, or is this, too, insight on his part? We may never know, if Greg doesn't think it important to spend time asking and discussing the matter. But then again, do we need to know?

But when an initial attempt at standing failed, Bert took it on his own to revert to a past failed approach.

Did the pastor spend too much time teaching about discipline? Were all of his points relevant to his counselees? Did they seem to profit from his "lecture?" Should he have engaged them in more discussion of each principle, or is what he did exactly what they needed?

The fact that Sue walked out on Bert is reminiscent of her behavior in a former counseling session. Should Greg have taken her up on this and discussed the matter in depth? Or was it enough for her to have to admit it? And did she ask forgiveness? Is this a pattern – doing wrong, then asking for forgiveness? Both counselees have learned a great deal so far. But has Bert learned as much about forgiveness as Sue?

Once more, Sue shows a fundamental desire to heed whatever God says in His Word. The mere reading of Ecclesiastes and Proverbs about immediacy of punishment convinces her. This is a good tendency on her part. It should be noted and encouraged, don't you think? If so, how?

There has been a breakthrough. Things have changed. There is a little hesitancy left, but it is more easily dealt with. There is a willingness to learn. So there is opportunity to teach. There is much more cooperation. Things are moving faster. Does this mean that counseling is drawing near to the end? Or is it merely an indication that though there is a lot to be done, it will probably take place much more rapidly? Did Greg drop a hint that counseling might end in the near future? What was it?

Counseling is going well. Let's hope there are no more setbacks! By the way, what would Sue have done if Bert continued to stand and said nothing?

Did Greg get sidetracked when he did not explore the post-argument situation any more fully than he did? Or was it better, at this point, to assume that they already understood their faults as, indeed, they seem to be doing regularly?

Let's continue…

Sue: I'd probably have felt stupid watching him stand there saying nothing and eventually would have told him to sit down so we could go on talking.

Pastor: You got it! Now, Bert, do you see the importance of standing rather than talking when there is an altercation? What you say and when you say it are both important. Proverbs 22:23 says, "He who guards his mouth and his tongue keeps himself from troubles."

Bert: Yeah. I was foolish to think I could solve the problem by arguing with her.

Pastor: Sue, what did you do when you calmed down?

Sue: I asked his forgiveness.

Pastor: Bert, did you forgive Sue?

Bert: Yes. I know I'm not to bring it up again to use against her. When I forgave her, I made that promise. As I think about it, I suppose I should have asked her for forgiveness over my failure to keep the standing rule. Sue, will you forgive me?

Sue: Of course.

Pastor: Good. That's settled. It seems that you've both learned the basic facts about forgiveness. Now, tell me what happened next?

Bert: Well, we settled down and had another go at it. Though we couldn't agree, we spoke *civilly* (ha ha!). We didn't write things up as you suggested, but we were prepared to tell you what happened.

Pastor: Do you think that you will be able to present a united front before the boys about the two rules you agreed on?

Bert: Absolutely.

Sue: I want to work hard on doing so. But I still don't trust myself. Suppose I fail and yell rather than punish them as I told them I would? What then?

Pastor: That gives you an opportunity to teach *them* something about forgiveness.

Sue: How so?

Pastor: Well, you ask them to forgive *you*. There is no more powerful force for teaching them what forgiveness is all about than to demonstrate it. Of course, you will not stage such a situation merely to teach. It has to be genuine. I can almost guarantee you that plenty of occasions will arise for both you and Bert to do so. Once you receive their forgiveness, punish them according to what you determined. Can't you just see their eyes grow large as they hear you say, "Boys, I was wrong to yell at you. That wasn't part of the punishment that we attached to this sin. I sinned too. Will you forgive me?"

Bert: I can see them right now! Wow, why didn't we conclude that this was the way to go long before this?

Pastor: How much Bible study do you do? And what sorts of Bible study books do you have? More Bible study would help a great deal. Then you'd know more about what God wants you to do before stumbling into wrong ways that displease Him. Remember how much your reading of Proverbs has already done for your thinking and acting.

Sue: How should we go about it? Are there any special books or programs that you would suggest?

Pastor: Yes, certainly. After this session, we'll go into the bookstore and I'll show you some books that would be helpful.

Bert: Good idea. I've roamed about the bookstore looking at them, but never knew which ones to purchase.

Sue: I'll look forward to it. If you could suggest one that has to do with mothers-in-law, that would be helpful.

Pastor: Oh? Do you have a problem there?

Bert: You bet we do.

Sue: You can say that again.

Pastor: Tell me about it.

Sue: Well there are two things that especially bug me...

Pastor: No. No. Nothing another person does should bug you – you bug yourself by responding wrongly. If you handled matters biblically, you wouldn't be bugged.

Sue: Okay. I see your point. It's just like when you told Bert about things that supposedly galled him.

Pastor: Right. Now go ahead. Tell me what you were going to say before I interrupted.

Sue: Well, there are two things that I bug myself about. How's that…? You see, Bert's mother lives two blocks away from us. So she's always coming over to our house. When she does, she is always trying to run our lives. She comes over and tells Bert what to think and do; and most of the time he listens to her. The second thing is that she's a Charismatic who is always getting a "prophetic word" to reinforce what she tells us to do. She's always "sensing" or "feeling" something or other from God.

Pastor: Before we get to these two matters, let me observe that in the last minute-and-one-half you used the word "always" four times!

Sue: Touche! The "language of exaggeration" as I think you called it?

Pastor: Exactly. We both know that this doesn't happen "always." Keep on telling yourself that it does and you will believe it. Now, for those two issues. We don't want to talk about your mother-in-law; she's not here. What's crucial is how you handle things when she says things you disagree with. After all, since she's not here, there's nothing we can do to help her. But you are here, so we must focus on what you should do. First, let me ask you, Bert, *Do* you allow your mother to tell you what to do in your marriage?

Bert: Sometimes.

Sue: Sometimes? How about alw… I mean very frequently?

Bert: Probably too often. But sometimes she's right.

Pastor: It's not wrong to listen to her advice, but you have become the head of a new decision-making unit, and – as the head – you are responsible for what you do. You no longer have to obey her. So if you let her influence your action by pressure or by supposed "words of knowledge," or the like, that's wrong. You and your wife are to make decisions on your own without bending to outside pressure. Do you remember Genesis 2:24?

Bert: Not off hand. What is it?

Pastor: It's God's answer to your problem. God says that a man shall leave his father and his mother, and be joined to his wife; and they shall become one flesh. Did you ever hear that before?

Bert: Yeah. Of course.

Pastor: You see it's the *man* who must make a clean break because of his headship. "Leaving" means that he is no longer under the authority of his parents. It's interesting in light of this verse that all of the mother-in-law jokes are about the husband's mother-in-law. You've never heard one about the woman's mother-in-law, have you?

Bert: No. But I never thought about that before.

Pastor: Well, let's think a bit about it now. Why do you suppose there are no mother-in-law jokes about the woman's mother-in-law? I'll tell you – because that's no joking matter! Two women pulling a man in opposite directions is not very pleasant for anyone. You and Sue argue about this, don't you?

Bert: Quite frequently.

Pastor: Then, it's time for you to go to your mother and tell her in a kindly way that you are the head of a new family. Also tell her that, while happy to hear her suggestions, you will make your own decisions and not be persuaded to act as she wants simply because of who she is. And assure her that you will no longer allow any undue pressure or influence to interfere with your home life.

Sue: Wow! If he only would!

Pastor: How about it, Bert?

Bert: I don't know. Wouldn't that hurt her?

Pastor: She shouldn't be hurt if she handles what you say as a Christian should. We don't act on the basis of whether others take offense at what we do, but on the basis of whether or not it is what God wants us to do. Second, doesn't all the hurt that comes to your marriage because you allow this situation to persist count for anything? And do you think that your mother is pleased when she sees you struggle with whom to listen to? Bert, if you do this thing, she may act hurt, not speak for a time, or something else, but you will please God and bring peace to your marriage. Are you going to do it?

Bert: With fear and trembling, but only because God says to.

Sue: Oh, Bert!

Pastor: There's no better reason for doing anything. Tonight, go home and at your conference table work on just how, when, and where to pull this off. Now, let's get to the Charismatic problem. Since this has been an especially long and tense session and tonight we are going to look at the church bookstore anyway, I will introduce you to a book that will help you sort things out for yourself. It's called, *The Christian's Guide to Guidance*. And when you've finished that one, I suggest you read a second, *Signs and Wonders in the Last Days*.

Sue: We'll buy them both!

Pastor: You know your homework, don't you? Okay. I'll accept your nods for "yes." Now let's pray. [They do, and head for the bookstore.]

Let's pause to discuss...

This was a hard, but productive, session. Hard ones often are. But did Greg attempt too much? Given the "leads" he had, could he have done otherwise? Will Bert do what he must do? He faced his boss and confessed sin. When he goes to his mother, ought he not confess wrong to her and ask forgiveness for not following Genesis 2? He should keep Romans 12:18 in mind as he goes.

And how about also confessing to Sue? Will they think about forgiveness at the conference table when they decide *how* to pull it off? It seems as if Greg is leaving them to the

Spirit in the application of Scripture to these matters. Are there ever times to do so? Not to do so?

How was it that Greg could tackle such subjects during this session when he couldn't before? Was it because there had been a breakthrough? If so, what brought about the breakthrough and how did it influence his boldness?

What did you think about Greg's suggestion about seeking forgiveness from the children? If Bert and Sue do so, will it undermine their authority with them? Or, on the other hand, will it more firmly establish it? Does it matter since it's the right thing to do?

Did you notice how Greg tied dealing with Bert's mother to Bert's becoming head of the home? In Bert's case, this motivation ought to be a very high one. Why?

Finally, was Greg wise in not taking on the Charismatic issue but relegating its discussion to two books? And why is Sue so anxious to buy both books?

Was this a good session or did it move too rapidly? Is Greg choking them with too many facts? Is he expecting too much from them too soon? Will Sue help Bert in his decision to talk to his mother? If so, how? What details of his imminent visit should they discuss at the conference table? Will they agree? Could it be that, in order to avoid the confrontation with Bert's mother, Greg might create a problem at the conference table that will prevent or postpone going?

Much to think about. But also something to pray about – especially the proposed visit.

SESSION EIGHT

Greg could hear them all of the way down the hall from his study even with the door closed. Though he couldn't make out their words, the lively discussion in which Bert and Sue were engaged seemed spirited, if not hostile. He wondered what he would encounter when the door opened. As they entered without knocking, they were still talking. Bert was firmly insisting, "I told you I did," and Sue was responding with equal firmness, "But you didn't. I know you didn't."

They quieted down and took their seats. But they were by no means calm. Bert had trouble sitting still as his hands nervously clasped and unclasped the arms of his chair, and Sue kept swinging her leg back and forth defiantly. When nothing more was said…

Greg announced: Welcome to counseling 101! What has gotten into you two? You sound like you are ready to explode any minute now. Calm down and tell me what's going on, please.

Sue: He says he did, but he knows that I know better. Why won't he tell the truth?

Pastor: What are you talking about?

Bert: I told her that I went to see my mother last night and did as you said, but she won't believe me.

Sue: But there's no reason to believe him. He left at 7 and returned at 7:25, and he had to walk the blocks between our houses! Come on! I wasn't born yesterday: there's no way he could have done that in so short a time. I think he went for a walk and then returned and didn't talk to her at all!

Bert: But I did. I did. It didn't take long to say what I had to say, and by the way Mom answered, I thought it was the better part of valor to leave quickly. So I did. It doesn't take any time at all to go and come a couple of blocks – especially when you cut through Mr. Merriman's lot!

Sue: Liar!

Pastor: Hold it, Sue! You know there's no place for that sort of talk in these sessions.

Sue: But he lied! He lied to me.

Bert: I didn't lie. I didn't.

Pastor: Well, it seems like we have to get to the bottom of this if we're going to get anywhere else tonight. Sue, why is it that you don't take Bert's word for it? Is there some solid reason for doubting him?

Sue: Well, there's the time factor. And…probably even more to the point, the way in which he nonchalantly strolled back into the house! No way! No way! I don't believe a word he's saying. He refused to see her all week, and then, at the last minute when it was easier to avoid having to talk about the visit, he pulls this stunt!

Bert: Look, pastor. I admit I was gutless and put off seeing her till the last moment. But I did go. I really did!

Pastor: What about this supposed "nonchalant" attitude?

Bert: I wasn't nonchalant. I simply kept my mouth shut and walked away because as soon as I stepped through the door Sue accosted me shouting, "You didn't go! You didn't! I know you didn't!" What was I to say? What *could* I say? She didn't believe me, and she was out of control and ranting and raging. How could I expect to be heard over that? How would I be believed, no matter what I said?

Pastor: Sue, do you have any more evidence than what you've offered so far – the time element, putting the encounter off till the last moment, and the nonchalant attitude?

Sue [noticeably calmer]: Well, don't you think that's enough? *I* do.

Pastor: I'm afraid I don't, and I'll tell you why: you are expressing an unloving attitude toward Bert. In I Corinthians

13:7 – the love chapter – Paul writes that love "believes all things, hopes all things...." Your evidence isn't solid; it's based on mistrust, fear and doubt.

Sue: But, pastor, I...

Pastor: Hold off for a minute, Sue. Let me finish. If love believes and love hopes (that is, *expects* the best), then belief and expectation triumph over suspicion. Now, if you consider the facts that you've presented, I think on a calmer appraisal of them that you'll see that there's no firm reason for you to doubt Bert's word. Let's look at those facts for what they are.

First, is it possible for someone to walk between your houses and back (taking the short cut) and still talk to someone for say 5 to 10 minutes?

Sue [reluctantly]: Just barely.

Pastor: Then, you admit that it *is* possible to do so. Okay, let's examine the next fact: the nonchalant attitude you noticed. Could you have misinterpreted it?

Sue: I don't see how I could have! He came...

Pastor: But is it *possible* that you did?

Sue: Of course it's possible! But I know Bert, and...

Pastor: So it *is* possible.

Sue: I suppose so, but...

Pastor: Now, just a minute until we take a look at the third piece of "evidence" you presented – the fact that Bert put off the encounter until the last minute. Then, I'll let you say all you want. Is it possible that a person dreading an encounter will put it off?

Sue: But I kept telling him all week to do it, and he just wouldn't. Can't you see that proves what I'm saying?

Pastor: No. And as a matter of fact, looking on this more objectively than either of you, I must say that. Furthermore, it's more likely that he put it off out of fear of the consequences. That *is* possible, isn't it?

Sue: All you keep saying is that something else is "possible." What's that got to do with the facts I presented?

Pastor: Everything! Unless these contrary explanations are not possible, then your case doesn't hold up. You've admitted that two are possible, and though you haven't answered my question about the third, I think that down deep inside you know it's possible as well. Am I right?

[No answer.]

Pastor: Okay. If you need time to think about it, that's fine. I can talk to Bert for a while. Bert, tell me exactly what happened.

Bert: There's nothing complicated about it. I walked over to my Mom's house, told her what you had said to tell her, and when she blasted off like a rocket, I got out fast. I may have looked nonchalant, but I was afraid to tell Sue what Mom said about her, so I may have walked into the house slowly enough that it could be interpreted as "strolling" in.

Sue: What did she *say* about me?

Bert: I thought that you didn't believe I was there. If I wasn't, then how could she have said anything?

Sue: But if you were, then you'd be able to tell me.

Pastor: Now, it seems we've reached a dilemma. On one side of it, Sue believes that Bert didn't go, on the other she wants to know what happened when he did. It's kind of like the man who said, "I didn't break the vase because I never had it, and I want you to know it was already broken when I got it." Now, Sue, please relax, think logically, and let's reason together.

Sue [sullenly]: Say what you've got to say.

Pastor: Thank you. Now, let's go back and look at the facts. All three of your charges can be explained differently and reasonably. You have presented no solid evidence for your contention that Bert lied about going. Was that a loving thing to do – according to the verse I just mentioned? Even if Bert *did* lie (which hasn't been established), shouldn't you give him the benefit of the doubt until such a time as the facts *prove* otherwise? Not to do so is to act on suspicion alone. And to accuse someone of lying on that ground is unloving. Now, go ahead, Sue, say whatever you want to say.

Sue: Grummph!

Pastor: What was that? I'm afraid I didn't get it.

Sue: I said "Grummph." That's what I said. And that's what I mean!

Pastor: Well, what *does* that mean? I don't understand.

Sue: It means a lot of things – for starters, it means that I believe you men are ganging up on me.

Pastor: Do you really think that? Or do you simply feel uncomfortable because you've been pushed into a corner?

Sue: Grummph!

Pastor: Well, because you're speaking a language I've never studied, I can't interpret what you're saying. So until we can converse in English again, I'll talk to Bert. Bert, what did your Mom say? Just tell me in calm terms, with any rough talk excluded, please.

Let's pause to discuss...

What to do or say now? Sue won't talk. She isn't making sense. She's utterly irrational. Does she see that her accusation is unfounded and that the problem is in her, or does she really think Greg and Bert are ganging up on her? That can often be a put-off rather than anything more. If Greg had wanted to (and who knows, he may have to) show her that this accusation was also unfounded and that it was, at best, mere suspicion, he could have done so devastatingly. But perhaps that's why he didn't. Sue was already on the ropes; perhaps Greg didn't care to administer the knockout blow!

At any rate, Greg's up to his neck in thick soup. How will he handle the situation? So far, he's been quite straightforward. Will he lose Sue because of this? Could or should he have been more diplomatic? Will Sue take off again? Before, her grunts (which are slightly different this time) always signaled that she was about to depart. So far, that isn't the case this time. Is there hope in that?

Not much has been done in this session so far. It seems that what is happening is setting things back – or is it? Can Greg pull it out of the fire and even turn it into a blessing? A large task! But let's see.

Now, it's time to hear from Bert. Will what he says be convincing – even to Sue? After all, she never gave him time to tell his story before accusing him of lying.

Let's continue...

Bert: What I said, in effect, was that I had been a wimp all my married life rather than the head of my home, that Genesis says that I should "leave" the authority of my father and mother, and that, while I would welcome advice, I would no longer allow *anyone* to meddle in our private affairs. Then, before I could say anything more, she told me off in non-Charismatic terms! You don't want to hear what they were. She blasted Sue, she blasted me, and, when I told her that we had been to see a biblical counselor who agreed with this, she blasted you!

Pastor: Well, thanks for sparing the non-Charismatic language! Now, Bert, in a day or two, as soon as you have an opportunity – when things have quieted down a bit – please tell your Mom that I am inviting her to attend a special counseling session with the four of us to talk about this. Do you think she'd come?

Bert: I don't know. She said a few choice things about you being anything but "biblical." I like your idea of meeting together, and if she'd come, it would be helpful I think. I'll do it.

Sue: I'd like to be there at that one!

Pastor: I invited you too. I am expecting you to come. Now, Sue, let's stop this foolishness. Listen to reason instead. If Bert has told you the truth, you are sure to know it as soon as you meet up with his Mom, don't you think? Is she likely to be all sweetness and light? Won't she have a good deal to say about his visit? Surely, in the light of his mother's response, there isn't any way Bert could get away with a lie like the one you've charged him with? Right?

Sue: Well......

Pastor: You do see that this is all uncalled for, and that the truth will soon surface after a day or two without you lifting a finger to help it. Mom's attitude toward Bert and you – and me – will make it perfectly clear whether Bert's lying or telling the truth. Can't you see that?

Sue: Ummmm. I hate to admit it, but that sounds logical. I guess – no, I think – I've probably been too emotional about this whole thing. But when I begged Bert to go, again and again, and he wouldn't, I was sure that he said so but didn't. Okay. You're right. I'd know as soon as I met his Mom. I *was* "foolish" as you said, pastor. I'm sorry for sinning this way. Bert, will you please forgive me?

Bert: Oh Sue! I'm so glad you believe me. Of course I'll forgive you. And though I haven't said so for a long while now, I just want to tell you that I love you.

Sue [now sobbing]: I... [sniff] I think I've been a fool! [drying her eyes with a tissue from her purse, and blowing her nose, Sue continues] I love you too!

[Bert takes her into his arms and kisses her.]

Pastor [sniffing a little himself]: I'm going into the other room and leave you two alone for a few minutes. You don't need a third party listening in. [He does.]

Let's pause to discuss...

Talk about turnarounds: this is one for the books! Here we were wondering whether Sue would leave, whether or not the session would go anywhere, and if Greg had pushed too far. He *was* firm, and very straightforward. Someone whose emotions are ruling her needs firm structure; Greg provided it. And it paid off.

Now, what of all of this emotion? Is it *only* emotion? Release of tension? Temporary? There's plenty of it to go around – even Greg is sniveling at the nose. But lying beneath all of the emotion, have we reached a layer of solid granite? Has the emotion released cleared the way for reality? Time will tell of course, but for now this must be taken for what it purports to be. Greg would be *un*wise to do *other*wise – wouldn't he? This doesn't seem like an occasion for questioning the validity of what transpired, but an opportunity to build on it.

What will Greg find when he returns to the room ten minutes later? And how will he handle it? Will he run with the change, will he caution about too much groundless hope placed in feelings rather than genuine life change stemming from the heart? How will he play it? It seems that the outcome of this emotional event lies in the direction he will take. Let's look in as Greg returns.

Let's continue...

[Greg enters to find that Bert and Sue have pulled their chairs close together and that they are holding hands. Their faces are fairly lit up. He sits down and begins.]

Pastor: What a change! You look like two new people!

Bert: We are, pastor. We are.

Sue: Yes, and we're truly grateful that you insisted on us – especially me – facing the facts. Now, we have a proposal to make to you. Tell him, Bert.

Bert: Gladly. We want you to marry us again.

Pastor [thunderstruck]: But…but I can't do that. You're already married.

Sue: That's true, but isn't there some way we could start anew that is like being married again?

Pastor: Well…

Bert: We want to take our vows again.

Pastor: You can certainly reaffirm the promises you made. We could do that if you really want to.

Bert and Sue: I do.

Pastor: That answer sounded like you almost did it! Well, I think that we've done enough for this session, so I'll get my book with the marriage ceremony questions and I'll ask them again. You're sure that you want to do this? [Both vigorously nod "yes."] Okay. Now, just before we do, let me ask one question. How has your homework been going? How about trash, socks, good meals, not assailing Bert as he comes from work, rules for the children, and your use of the conference table?

Bert: In spite of the tension of the week, everyone of those matter, with the exception of the conference table, has continued.

Pastor: Rules beginning to work for the children?

Bert: We made and explained the rules to them in a sort of ceremony and have been sticking to the proper penalties as agreed. The kids are beginning to see that we mean business, and though not 100%, we're beginning to see results.

Pastor: Good.

Sue: I thought that just in case something should happen to help us move toward a biblical marriage, I'd better not let up on my homework, even though it was hard when I couldn't convince Bert to go see his mother earlier in the week. Now I'm glad that I stayed with it.

Pastor: I'm glad you did, too. But at our next meeting, I expect to hear good things about how you are beginning to use the conference table effectively. For one thing, you can begin talking about what changes the vows you are about to make again today will mean for the future of your marriage. Write down whatever answers you can agree upon. And add some possible ways and means to bring about each of the proposed changes. You should be ready to support each of these desired changes by biblical reasons for it. And one more thing before we listen to those vows – don't get cocky. You've done well tonight, but you have a good bit yet to accomplish. The gains that you've made must be solidified. I'm sure that you remember I Corinthians 10:13 since I've stressed it so often; at your conference table tonight, read the verse immediately before it – I Corinthians 10:12. Now, I'll go get my book. [Greg does, the vows are taken again, and what happens thereafter is simply none of our business!]

Let's pause to discuss…

How well did Greg handle the situation? Should he have stretched it out further, instructing, warning, and encouraging them? Possibly. But would it have taken away from the moment? And in such a flood of emotion, how much would have been heard and retained? Yet he does show concern about solidifying what has taken place, and lets them know that a breakthrough of this sort isn't an end but, rather, the beginning of such a solidifying period. He even starts them thinking about this by assigning the reading of I Corinthians 10:12.

As always, Greg is faithful to check up on homework –
even in the midst of elation, turmoil, and confusion. He even
assigns new work for them.

I don't know how this has affected you, but clearly Greg
has been caught up into the emotion, while at the same time,
remembering his role as a counselor and not only as a loving
friend and pastor.

What do future sessions hold? And how many will there
be? This is the eighth. One of those, however, was only a half
session. Greg must consider this matter of time carefully. Will
he hover over them during the rooting and grounding period,
or will he set them loose with proper structure and instruction about how to work on their own? Obviously, that is a
crucial question that is running through Greg's mind. He
hasn't yet settled it, but at least by the next session he should
have a pretty good idea about what to do. Perhaps the decision
will hang upon what happens at the ninth session. We'll see.

And...will "Mom" agree to a session? If so, it will be
interesting. If nothing else, such a session should serve to
firm up Bert's resolution, especially if it turns out well. An
additional session will mean that Greg will be in for something else he hadn't originally planned upon. But he showed
flexibility in proposing the extra side-session, and now he
must continue to be flexible if it takes place. Let's hope that it
occurs. If it does, let's pray that it will help, not hinder, counseling for Bert and Sue.

Session Eight–A

[It was only two evenings later when Bert, Sue, Mrs. Brown (Bert's mother), Greg, and the Holy Spirit met for counseling. Greg led the session as best he could.]

Pastor: It's good to see you all here tonight. I'm especially happy that you decided to come, Mrs. Brown. Now, let's think for a moment about why we are here.

As I understand it, Bert came to see you three nights ago to tell you of a recent decision he made. Is that correct?

Brown: Correct and incorrect! Correct that he came, incorrect that he should have come and that he said what he said! And you were a part of it, I gather. Right?

Pastor: I did counsel with Bert and Sue and…

Brown: You certainly did! You counseled my son not to have anything more to do with me. As you know, I'm a widow, he's my only child, and I have no one else. How could you do such a thing?

Bert: Mom. You've got it all wrong. He did no such thing. He has been helping us put our marriage back together, and part of what I have had to do is to stop being such a wimp and take responsibility for my family.

Brown: You no longer consider *me* family? Has that wife of yours been coming between us again, wanting you all for herself?

Sue: I've done no such thing! Ever since we've been married, you've wanted Bert to remain a little boy that you could order around at your command. And whenever it looks like you might not get your way, you whine and cry until he gives in – even when he knows that he shouldn't. Why…

Pastor: Now, let's calm down and try to think this matter through biblically. Mrs. Brown, you do understand that the passage in Genesis that Bert referred to when he came to see you requires a man to "leave his father and mother" when he marries and to "cleave to his wife," don't you?

Brown: Young man, I've forgotten more Bible than you'll ever know! Of course I do. But it doesn't mean to separate one's self entirely from his family.

Pastor: Of course it doesn't. But it does speak of breaking a temporary relationship for the sake of establishing a permanent one. Parents have authority over their children only for a time – then, when their children marry they become part of a new decision-making unit with its own authority and responsibilities. Bert left your home physically, but he never left in heart and mind. Now, he has determined to put his wife before anyone other than the Lord and to allow no one else to come between them. That may be hard to take, but in the long run it will bring greater peace and harmony between you and Bert and Sue. You see…

Brown: Quiet! Ah, yes. Yes…Yes…Yes, Lord. I see. Thank You Lord. Thank you! Hallelujah! Praise the Lord!

Sue: What was that all about?

Brown: You and your Presbyterian crowd wouldn't understand if I told you.

Pastor: Try us. Tell me about it.

Brown: Alright! I just received a word of knowledge telling me not to listen to anything you say…that you don't understand the Bible…that you are of the devil. And that I should leave this minute – which I intend to do. [She gets up, swirls about, and sashays through the door with her head held in the air.]

Pastor: I'm very sorry for you that this happened and for her. We could have worked out a much better relationship for you all if she would only listen.

Bert: Normally, I would have gone after her, pleading with her. But now, I see that it's best for us all that I don't cater to that sort of behavior on her part any longer.

Sue: That's the kind of good news that I've been waiting to hear for a long time.

Pastor: You see, don't you, how she used her Charismatic claims to come to her defense? Just as soon as she began to hear what she didn't want to hear, she supposedly received a revelation to leave. God surely didn't tell her that we, who have trusted Christ as Savior, are "of the devil." That, in itself, demonstrates that there was no revelation from God.

Sue: But do you think she really heard something?

Pastor: No. She attempted to manipulate us by what she did.

Bert: What do we do now?

Pastor: Just continue what you have already started doing – become a responsible, loving family unit that properly relates to others, including your mother. You should act normally toward her, treat her with respect, pray for her, and do good to her. But you must not let her run your lives or interfere with your home any longer. If you do that, and if you don't give in to future intimidation or manipulation – of whatever kind – I predict that in time she'll come around. How soon, it's hard to say.

Bert: I hope so.

Sue: That poor woman. I feel sorry for her. She's right. She has no one else but us. And now she thinks that we've alienated ourselves from her. We've got to work at building a new, loving, and proper Christian relationship with her.

Pastor: Well said. And, having said that, what more is there to say? Let's pray. [All three do, especially praying for Mom's welfare.]

Let's pause to discuss…

What a failure! Or was it? You know the audience can be a failure even when the play is a success. Remember the ten lepers who came to Jesus? Only one returned. Were Jesus' efforts a 9 to 1 failure? Certainly not!

Then, who failed here?

Not Sue. She spoke well, and gained a new concern for Mom Brown that could blossom into something fine in days to come, now that the barrier between her and Mom has been destroyed.

Not Bert. Hard as it must have been, he stuck to his guns and refused to be intimidated.

Greg? Possibly. Could he have done better? Was he too undiplomatic? Or was his approach exactly what Mom needed?

Mrs. Brown? Definitely. Not that, given her habit patterns in relationship to Bert, she acted out of character. Such behavior could have been expected. Greg probably did anticipate something of the sort. But could it have been helped? Probably not. To prolong matters any more than he did would simply have been agony for all.

What about the "word of knowledge?" Because Greg and Sue read the books about gifts that Greg recommended, they were fortified against Mom Brown's attempt to manipulate them. And what's new? She's supposedly received direct, divine revelation before.

What did you think of Greg's analysis of the phenomenon? Could Mom have really thought she heard those words? Sue wonders about that. It's very unlikely. She probably rehearsed them all the way over to herself – not necessarily as a word of knowledge, but as her appraisal of the situation. If she "heard" anything, it was her own inner voice speaking to her, repeating what she believed.

Well, we may or may not hear anything more about Mrs. Brown, but Bert and Sue have a task ahead of them that they must pursue to the end. And at the conclusion of the session Sue expressed it as well as, or even better than, Greg could have.

SESSION NINE

[Counseling is back on schedule after the special session with Mrs. Brown. Greg is concerned to see how, after a few more days, Sue and Bert are handling the outcome. So he throws out a line that will not prejudice their answers.]

Pastor: Good to see you both. That was quite a time together a couple of days ago, wasn't it?

Bert: No doubt about that! But despite the ruckus, it was a freeing experience for me. I've been a new person ever since. To be able to break a hold that should never have existed and to have been able to firmly cement one that I should have long ago is wonderful. I feel sorry for Mom, and I love her still. But I allowed her to become a detriment to our marriage. Now, we must work on building a proper relationship with her.

Pastor: Sounds like the session together wasn't entirely a failure then. How about you, Sue?

Sue: For years, I've almost loathed Mom for the part she played in pulling Bert away from me. I've been resentful, and that's hurt me and Bert and our relationship. Since the matter has come out in the open this way, I've confessed my resentment to God and I have a new hopeful outlook on the future. I don't think I realized how much this issue was weighing me down. I've been thinking about ways in which my attitude hindered developing a proper relationship with Mom so that when she calms down and is finally willing to see me, I can ask for her forgiveness. I tried to talk to her after the session, but she won't answer the phone or come to the door. I know she's all right, though, because she's been phoning all over the neighborhood to tell her cronies – I mean her friends – all about our encounter. Truthfully, I feel sorry for her. She's a miserable, lonely person. If only she'd come to you for counseling, I think you could help her.

Pastor: Well, I'd be glad to minister to her, but – at least at the moment – that idea doesn't seem viable. Perhaps after you work out a new and better relationship with her, she will be amenable to the idea. Since the issue is before us, let me say that a crucial part of your three-per-week conference tables should be the determination of ways to build the new relationship with Mom. May I suggest that you begin by *showing* love. We once talked about that. Do you remember what love is?

Bert: Giving.

Sue: Giving her something she needs that we have.

Pastor: Great! You've got it. It doesn't necessarily have to be some *thing*. Though it might be. When you do, she may think you're trying to "make up" with her, but don't let that deter you. If you persist, she'll soon find out that you are doing what you do because you care. Sue, just don't let your warmer feelings for her get the better of you so that you begin to do what Bert used to do.

Sue: Thanks for the heads up. I have been feeling very sorry for her.

Pastor: Okay. Now to your homework. How about trash, socks, meals, greetings at door, time with the children on Saturdays, rules and penalties? Is all continuing well in spite of intervening events?

Bert: The things that you assigned us have made such a difference in our home that we wouldn't dare let up on such productive homework.

Pastor: I gather that means you are keeping up in *all* areas?

Sue: He's telling the truth. That's exactly how good we feel about the homework. It's the thing that has made the difference. Reading and praying together daily, and at the conference table, has also been rewarding. I believe – not "guess" – that God is going to give us a marriage that sings. There are moments when I see how Bert's changed that I do hum a little tune!

Pastor: I'm happy that you appreciate homework because I'm about to give you some more. This week, go back to each of your original lists of ways in which you are failing God as a person, spouse, or parent, and from each list, choose two more small, concrete items (like trash and socks). Then, decide at the conference table what to do about them, and begin doing it. Next week I'm going to want to know what they were and how you are coming with them. Bert, do you remember your special list of things to do for Sue? Well, take one more of those, one that is of the highest priority of those left, and start doing whatever it is without telling Sue which it is. It will be interesting to see if she detects what it is during the week.

Bert: Sounds like fun!

Sue: Sure does! Who'd ever think that counseling is fun? Well, of course, it hasn't all been fun I know. Pastor, could I do the same thing for Bert this week?

Pastor: By all means.

Bert: Sounds too good to be true!

Let's pause to discuss…

There has definitely been a breakthrough. Listen to the counselees. They are light-hearted; they are even having "fun." Is that dangerous? Is all of this good humor nothing more than an emotional binge? No way! Not when along with it they are working earnestly at changing their patterns of life. This indicates that it is the real thing! When emotion is *substituted for change,* it is unworthy. But these good feelings are the fruit of good works (see Genesis 4:7). And those good works are the fruit of the Spirit. Homework, as biblical counselors pursue it, is nothing more or less than the works discussed by James that grow out of authentic faith. A counselee learns what God's will is, believes that he should do it to please God, asks the Spirit for help in doing so, and then moves ahead to do it. It is as simple – and profound – as that.

Now, perhaps more emphasis should be placed upon how *God has blessed them.* Greg will certainly do so before terminating counseling. But when people are obeying the Scriptures, it is not essential all of the time to keep *telling* them that they are doing so to honor God. At the outset, you will remember that Greg strongly emphasized the work of the Spirit leading to works that please God. These counselees have caught on to that. The proof of this is in the pudding that has replaced the "soup!"

Has Greg thrown too much homework at them? If so, they will let him know next week. If it is too much, since they appreciate what it means that works must grow out of faith, and since the results that appertain thereto have been so productive of blessing, they are more likely to "kill themselves trying." Even if they don't do everything, they will do much. We can almost count on that. If he discovers that it was too much on top of what they have already been doing, then Greg can simply reduce the amount that he would have given the next time.

How much longer will counseling last? Every sign of a genuine breakthrough is apparent: no more foot dragging, joy, willingness to obey God, genuine God-honoring effort, generalizing of principles (note Sue's request to enter into the "fun"), ease of counseling, and so forth. There is *noticeable newness* in the counseling. That's the overall sign of a genuine breakthrough. For more on the breakthrough sessions (this one extended over a *couple* of sessions with multiple, smaller, prior breakthroughs), read *Critical Stages of Biblical Counseling*.

Well, what next? Will there be much more to discuss in this session? We shall see.

Let's continue...

Pastor: But it *is* true. And do you know why? Because God has given you His Word to obey, and by His Spirit – the Other Counselor in these sessions – has encouraged, strengthened, and enabled you to obey it. That's the truest thing in all the world.

Bert: Since I've been coming here, I've learned so much about the Scriptures and what God expects of us and does for us, I'm actually hungry for more. Is there some way that I can grow more quickly in my biblical understanding?

Pastor: Well, in two weeks we are beginning a ten-week study about what it means to be a church elder. It's a three-hour course, *every* Saturday without fail. All who register must promise to attend the entire ten-week course of study. While you are not ready to become an elder, but like others who are serious about their faith, you are invited to take that training anyway. It is of a nature that is helpful to all. It will not be filling in white spaces. It will not only stretch your mind but also focus on your life. Who knows, in time, you may become an elder or deacon. If so, this will give you a head start. Now, there's only one problem: this class meets on Saturday afternoon. Do you know why that presents a problem?

Bert: No. Why? – Oh, now I remember! That's when I take care of the kids.

Pastor: Right. Now, how are you going to resolve that problem?

Bert: Let me think. Hmmmmm? Tonight at the conference table I'll lay it before Sue to see what she thinks. Perhaps together, in one way or another, we can work it out. If not, I won't fudge on my responsibility to care for the children, no matter which way we resolve it.

Sue: No need! I already have a suggestion. I'll let you off the hook as long as the course continues. I want a husband who desires to know and live God's way. I'll gladly take care of the children while I know Bert's getting such instruction. But, pastor, do you have a *good* women's Bible study group I can attend? By "good" I mean those in which I can really learn the Bible and what it means for life. I want to become a wife that lives up to a husband who is taking eldership training.

Pastor: So glad you asked. No, at the moment we don't. I know that there are one or two women who from time to time have expressed the same desire, but we've never had enough to form a group. Tell you what. Hustle up a half dozen or more women in the church who, for the same reason, would like to become part of a group, and I'll get an elder to teach it. If I can't find one whose schedule is open, I'll teach it myself. How's that?

Sue: Oh, would you? That's wonderful!

Bert: It seems that we bit off a lot more than we anticipated when we decided to come for biblical counseling. It's amazing to discover what Christian counseling is like.

Pastor: Just remember, "not all that glitters is gold." There is counseling and there is counseling. The name "Christian" may or may not be a valid designation of any given counseling. Many – perhaps most – of those who *call* their counseling "Christian" or even "biblical" don't really counsel according to the Scriptures. The fact that Christians counsel doesn't make their counseling Christian. There are Christians who use the methods of non-Christians, meaning well, and thinking that they are correct. But their counseling is no more Christian or biblical than what goes on up the street at the secular counseling center. Truly biblical counseling, in contrast, grows out of and is consistent with the Scriptures at every point. You remember the remarks made to you about the "kook," that so many "professional" Christian counselors disagree with him? That's because their own counseling is not *biblical,* and he has exposed the fact. You can read more about these things in his writings, but let me lend you a small volume by him entitled, *Is All Truth God's Truth?* That will get you started. [Greg pulls a copy of it off the shelf and hands it to Bert.]

Bert: Thanks. I read his other books and profited from them. I'm sure this one will help as well.

Sue: Well, now that we're all fixed up, I suppose counseling is about to come to a conclusion?

Pastor: Yes and no. What did the verse I gave you from I Corinthians 10 last time have to say?

Sue: That we are to take care not to be overconfident.

Pastor: Good. I see that you read and understood it. That's the danger at this juncture. You are on a roll spiritually, and the tendency will be to think you've just about "made it" and therefore can let up. The opposite is true. You've learned some new biblical patterns of living, and you are beginning to appropriate them into your lives. Great! But all sorts of distractions may throw you off course if you allow them to do so. You must learn how to resist these, being especially careful to do so while the new patterns are becoming habitual to you. The question is this: how soon will you be prepared to go it alone?

Paul had a word about "going it alone" when writing to the Philippians. He said that the church was to obey God when he was absent (he was in jail) just as they did when he was present (2:12). They would have to work out the solution ("salvation"[1]) to the problem of disunity that had developed in the congregation *on their own*. There is a time for that, and it will soon come for you. When it does, it will be well to remember that you are not really alone: you don't need me or anyone else to help. Why? Because, as Paul went on to tell them, they were not really alone since God was with them, producing both the desire and the ability to please Him (v. 12). The question is this: when will you have learned the new ways of God and how to depend on Him to keep you walking in them fully enough to do so?

Sue: That's a big question, isn't it? In one sense, it frightens me to think we can't turn to counseling every week for help, but on the other hand, it cheers me to think that a time will come when we won't need to.

Bert; She just expressed my sentiments exactly!

Pastor: Well, then, enough for that. Now let's get down to work in this session. There is so much more to do.

---

1. Here, "salvation" refers not to eternal salvation (the Philippians were already believers), or to sanctification in general, but to the specific task of getting through a difficult situation (the church split) successfully (cf. Philippians 1:19).

Sue: You mean this session is only beginning?

Let's pause to discuss...

That's what you may have been thinking too. But there are some important matters yet to cover. As always, Greg seems to know where he wants to go and will anticipate and lead them to those places that breed confidence in him. But where does he want to go now? Think about it.

If you do think about it, you'll realize, for instance, that there is some summary teaching that is necessary. Throughout, he has been teaching, but it has always been embedded in some issue or pattern of change. As a result, this teaching may not have always appeared as sharply delineated as it might. Now, apart from the immediacy of using it, he can take time to summarize much of what they have been taught in a way that will make it even more memorable.

Next, Greg hasn't probed into some areas of their lives. He has had to focus on priorities so that there has been no time to do so. Now, he must go round the circle of their lives, probing other pieces of the pie. Of course, he can't take up every possible issue. Nor should he. Counseling is only a small portion of the sanctification process – one that kicks in when normal growth ceases in a Christian's life. It exists to break the log-jam and get sanctification flowing again. More generally speaking, sanctification, in this growth process, deals with the *other* growth areas.

Greg will be looking for larger items that, up until now, have been neglected. Since some of these may be lurking behind those that have emerged (as the mother-in-law problem was), they may require several more weeks of counseling. But on the other hand, if all else seems well – i.e., improvement (not always completion) is well on the way – he may want to close counseling very soon. Often improvement in one area sparks improvement in others (just as the opposite can be true). After all, we are whole persons: what affects us in one area of life also affects us in others.

Are there other matters to clear up? Issues to raise? Suggestions to make? Possibly. But as you can see, the matters that have just been mentioned are all end-of-counseling matters.

Let's continue…

Pastor: No, we're not beginning again, but we must continue on. I am concerned to know how things are going in some other areas of your lives beyond those that we have explored. We've dealt largely with the marriage and family area. Is there anything else there that we've missed?

Sue: Don't think so.

Bert: We've pretty well covered it.

Pastor: Okay. Now, what about work? We've handled the boss problem. Incidentally, he's sending his son for pre-counseling next week. One of our elders will be counseling him. You might continue to pray about that. But what about others at work – any problems there?

Bert: Not that I know of.

Pastor: How about friends, neighbors, other church members – any difficulties there?

Sue: No.

Pastor: Finances?

Bert: No problems.

Pastor: Sexual relations?

Sue: Resumed.

Pastor: Any other areas you'd like to suggest that we should cover?

Bert: Not at the moment. If some problem occurs that we don't anticipate, can we come back for further help?

Pastor: You're jumping the gun. I'll get into that in detail next week. But for now, is there anything else?

Bert: No.

Pastor: Then, let's begin summing up some of the biblical principles we've learned in counseling:

1. We learned that what we do we must do in order to please God – not to get relief.
2. We also learned that we must find God's will in the Bible – not in some other revelation…

Bert: Like a supposed "word of knowledge." By the way, I read those two books on guidance and gifts and really got help from them. I wish every Charismatic – including Mom – would read them!

Pastor: Who knows? Perhaps the time will come when she will be willing – after she comes to recognizes the good "Presbyterianism" has done for her and you. But now, here's another:

3. We learned that you must always sort out your responsibilities. Do you recall what that means?

Bert: Just a bit vague on that. Can you help me?

Pastor: Sue, do you remember?'

Sue: Like Bert, I'm not sure.

Pastor: When someone says, "Well, I'll do so-and-so *if* he or she will do thus and thus…"

Bert: Now I remember. You must do what God requires whether or not anyone else does what he should.

Sue: We must do it to please God, not to get some result out of another. Nor should we try to excuse ourselves on the basis that someone else isn't assuming his responsibilities.

Pastor: Couldn't have said it better myself! Let's take up just one more for now.

4. When a problem arises, we are not merely to pray about it, but should pray that God will give us the opportunity, wisdom, resources, and ability to do what He requires of us in His Word.

Sue: Right. And if a husband isn't doing as he should toward his wife, he can't expect his prayers to be answered (I Peter 3:7).

Bert [smiling broadly]: I can see that you learned that one well!

Pastor: It'll be good that she – and especially you – don't forget it. Now, Sue, we'll count that as #5. There are many more that we have encountered as counseling progressed, but we'll hold them till next time. Go home and chew on these. These biblical principles have gone a long way toward helping you both deal with the issues you have been struggling with. And if you have time, check out some of those principles that we learned from your favorite book, Proverbs. By the way, have you been reading a chapter of Proverbs every day?

Bert: Some days, not all.

Sue: Yeah. We need to get back into that practice.

Pastor: Good idea. Now that we've covered at least these items, let's pray and ask God's blessings on the week to come. If you can think of anything else that we should have covered, but didn't, write it out and bring it with you next week.

[They pray.]

Let's pause to discuss…

Well, Greg is moving rapidly. Even more so than we thought he would. That summing up process, for instance, is usually relegated to the last or next-to-last session. Could Greg think that counseling has turned the corner and is now on the last lap? Looks like it. Is he right?

Do you think that his counselees have become dependent upon him? If not, why not? If so, why so?

What do you think of the discussion of homework? How important was it to emphasize the way that it has affected counseling? Couldn't it be listed as #6? How many more principles can be added to the list? Will Greg cover them all? Will they remember them all, even if he does? Should they be listed for his counselees' memory?

Are they functioning well between sessions? Have they fully caught on to the process, willingly entered into it, and made it a part of their lives for the future? How will Greg know unless they completely fail? And we don't want that as an indicator, do we? What more is there to do in counseling? Surely, they need "rooting and grounding," but Greg has gone to lengths to tell them that they are not yet there and should be cautious about thinking they are "standing" when they are not. Is there more counseling to do in this regard?

Many more things may be running through Greg's mind, but he has reason to rejoice at what God has done so far through his counseling of Bert and Sue.

SESSION TEN

[All parties are gathered together for what, as only Greg knows, will be the last session if all is well.]

Pastor: The usual question: How did things go this week?

Sue: After last week's session, I can only say "splendid!"

Pastor: Bert?

Bert: Agreed! Indeed, very, very well.

Pastor: Sounds good. Tell me about your homework – all done as required?

Bert: Absolutely! Down to doing things that each other had to try to recognize. I caught Sue making special efforts to find ways of pleasing me. For instance, she listened to some of my favorite TV programs and didn't gripe that they were inane, and so on.

Pastor: Sue, what, exactly, did you set out to do?

Sue: Well, he got it. I tried to do little things when we were together that would please him. I'm glad that he noticed it. The TV matter was only one of several small things.

Pastor: Good. Now, Sue, what did you notice Bert doing?

Sue: Well, he helped clear the table, one day cleaned the windows, and on another worked in the garden. Basically, he attempted the same sorts of things I did.

Pastor: Well that's good! Now, how is the three-times-a-week conference table going? Still at it?

Bert: Wouldn't miss it for anything. It's *transformed* our relationship. We now talk instead of yell at or ignore one another.

Sue: We didn't meet one night because Billy was sick, and I had to care for him at that time. But it wasn't out of neglect. As a matter of fact, I missed it.

125

Pastor: How is Billy? Nothing serious, I hope.

Sue: He's okay now. Had a stomach upset – throwing up all over the house. Not very conducive to a quiet conference table!

Pastor: I'm glad you haven't become legalistic about such things, even though while in counseling I've insisted on consistency and regularity, but you have learned to be properly flexible. Since you've mentioned the children, let me ask how the rules are being followed.

Bert: Better and better. The house is getting into order. We deeply appreciate what you have helped us do there.

Pastor: Great! But of course, it's the Lord Who is behind every such change that takes place. Remember to praise Him. I'm but a minister; the word means "servant." As He enables me, it's my job to minister the Word of God and His job to enable you to fulfill its commands. I wouldn't have a thing to say or do if I didn't have His inerrant Bible to guide me as I counsel. Sometimes, I wonder how others can even undertake to counsel anyone without such a vital standard for life and godliness. Well, do you have anything else to tell me?

Bert: Not me.

Sue: Nor do I.

Pastor: I'm of the opinion that it's time to say "so long" for a while. More counseling at this point might be pointless, unproductive, and lead to unwanted dependence. You must come to depend on the Lord and the normal growth processes God has provided through His church from now on.

Bert: You don't mean it?

Sue: Ah! Graduation day!

Pastor: Yes and no. I said, "for a while." I meant by that phrase that I want to dismiss you now, but then see you in six weeks to be sure that all is continuing well. We're talking about checking *up*, not checking *out*. If, at that time, all is still going well, we can say "goodbye" to counseling permanently. How does that grab you?

Bert: Just right.

Sue: I was wondering how much longer counseling would last, but I thought it might continue one or two more weeks.

Pastor: Do you want it to?

Sue: Oh no. I just had that in mind as a genuine possibility. I'm glad things have come to an end.

Pastor: No. No. Not an end – a new beginning. The key thing to keep in mind is that these six weeks will be a *transition period*. Over that period, what you have learned will either solidify so that it should affect your lives for good, or you will regress. There is no reason for the latter to happen, and every reason to expect the former to take place. But the six-week checkup is designed to determine which it will be. If you do well, but need some fine-tuning, we might add a seventh week. If things go down hill, a longer number of additional sessions might be necessary. But I expect that all will go quite well and that we'll say "goodbye" after the six-week checkup.

Bert: Things have gone well so far; I expect that to continue.

Pastor: It should, but don't forget I Corinthians 10:12!

Sue: When we began counseling, I never dreamed that you would have arranged things so systematically. You certainly seem to know where you are going and what to do to get there. This six or seven-week checkup is only the latest example. Where did you learn all of this?

Pastor: Are you ready for this? I was trained under…

Sue: Don't tell me – the "kook!"

Pastor: You got it in one!

Bert: Amazing! And here we were criticizing the very man who helped you help us.

Pastor: Perhaps you can inform your Bible Study friend of your contacts with his books and his friend. Now, no more chitchat (though it is in place at this session). It's time to get to work.

Bert: Work discussed *here* almost always leads to work to do at *home*. (Notice I didn't say "always.") Though so far, it has been true every time.

Pastor: Here is what you are to do during the next six weeks. You'll notice that I've printed it up on this form [which he extracted from his note folder and now shows them]. I want to read it after you've completed it, and if necessary, discuss it with you:

1. Keep up every homework assignment that you have been following without fail.

2. Hold regular conference table meetings.

3. Read Proverbs each day.

4. Each week, at the last of the three conferences for that week, give yourselves written homework for the week following. Use the large list or any other that you care to. Bring these homework assignment papers to the six-week checkup.

5. Also, at that time, bring a written evaluation of how well you did in following your assignments. Write these out at the conference table one week after giving the assignment.

6. Keep a clear and detailed record of any problems that arose during the six-week period and what, if anything, you did about them. Include a written evaluation of what happened.

7. If there are any other problems serious enough that you could not solve them and need help in doing so, place a star on the record next to them.

8. During the six-week period, do not, do *not*, I say, contact me about anything having to do with the transitional work that you are doing. Only in a *dire emergency* should you break that rule (please look up the word "dire" in your dictionary and you'll know what I'm talking about). That means not making phone calls, sending e-mails, writing letters, using smoke signals, or waving semaphore flags. I think you get the idea.

Sue [smiling at the last few words]: All too clearly.

Bert: Right! But we'll see you at church. What will we do then?

Pastor: Act as if you are no longer in counseling. You won't be, you know. You'll be in transition from counseling to normal Christian living.

Sue: Let me be sure why it is that you don't want us to contact you.

Pastor: Simply this – I want to see how well you can go it alone. If you depend on me rather than the Lord during that period, we will invalidate the test.

Sue: That's what I thought. Makes sense.

Pastor: Now is there anything else we need to discuss before you leave today?

Sue: Hmmmmm. No, I can't think of anything.

Bert: I can't either. But I do want to thank you for all you've done.

Pastor: You're more than welcome. But you're not through with me yet. Remember, we meet again in six weeks!

Sue: Let me echo Bert's words. It's been *the* experience of my life so far that I will remember most. Thanks.

Pastor: You're welcome. Now, let's pray.

Let's pause to discuss...

Short session! As it should be if there is nothing more to talk about. Besides, when a session focuses mostly on a single subject, as this one did, it's bound to be short. But thereby, it emphasizes that fact. Greg wanted to enlist them for the six-week transition period. That was his one object once he heard that there was no other pressing problem to consider. And he did give ample opportunity for them to say so, if there were.

What do you think of the detailed printed instructions that Greg handed them about the six-week transition? Sue and Bert seem impressed. Sue comments on the systematic way in which Greg conducts counseling, even before she hears about the transition period and reads the detailed instructions concerning it. You wonder, don't you, how much more that must have impressed her?

The six-week period gives the counselees a sense of security; should anything happen they will be able to report it at the end and get help. They are, therefore, only partially on their own ("transitioning," as Greg keeps on putting it). Obviously, he wants to give them a sense of freedom and security at the same time. Do you think that the transition period does that? Does it serve to break any undue dependence as well?

How well do you think Bert and Sue will do? Will there be but one more session? Two? Or even more? What are your predictions?

What, mostly, have you learned from this series of counseling sessions? Has it been of help? Are you interested in more books of the same sort, only focusing on other kinds of problems? If so, contact Greg or Jay through the publisher, and they may be able to provide them.

Until six weeks from now, goodbye!

THE SIX-WEEK CHECKUP

[Bert and Sue arrive with a notebook from which there is an envelope protruding. Greg notices it, but makes no comment.]

Pastor: Well, here we are again after all those weeks! That's a long time, isn't it? One in which you had the opportunity to let things gel or splash them all around. From the looks on your faces, I gather that your marriage has gelled up pretty well. Am I right?

Sue: You'd better believe it! This "transition" period was just what we needed. We would have been at a loss without it. We'd probably been at sea if you just dumped us. And we wouldn't have had anyone to hold us to working at things to solidify our gains. It was just what the doctor ordered!

Bert: Sue usually puts things better than I, but all I can say is that it's been the best forty days and forty nights of our lives!

Pastor: Sounds great. Now, let's get to work, and I hope this time it'll not mean homework after you leave! Were there any problems that you couldn't solve – ones that you starred?

Sue: Nothing serious came up. We dealt with a number of minor problems, but we have nothing to bring to you for help.

Pastor: Okay. Now, let me see your record. Is it in that notebook?

Bert [as he hands it to Greg]: Yes, we have a complete record of the homework we gave ourselves and how it turned out.

Pastor: Now let's see. Hmmmm. What does this mean? "Discuss books. Did so and found that we had learned much from them. Each had learned different facts that stood out. Shared these. Good times at conference table doing so." Now, what books are you talking about?

Sue: The books *Guidance* and *Signs and Wonders in the Last Days*. We had each read them separately, but never until now

131

had time to discuss them. It was interesting. We thought about all of the things that Mom had claimed to experience over the years and how often she had made poor decisions, and realized for the first time what was at the bottom of many of them. We determined that if God enables, we will help her see how the errors of her faith are destroying her life.

Pastor: Speaking of Mom, have you reestablished contact with her, and what is it like?

Bert: Yes, we have. You'll notice that the next item on the record is to work on it: "Regain Mom's confidence and love by showing love to her." We've been working on that. She was cold at first, but when we began to take her to the store, go places with her, spend time visiting, and so on, it made a lot of difference. There's still a long way to go, but we're going to persist until we win her over completely – and I hope that even means to become a member of Scriptural Pres!

Pastor: That would be a feat! But God bless you in the attempt. However, don't push too hard or too soon. Let it come naturally. Perhaps, when we have special programs at the church, you can invite her. Now, let's see, the item for week three is: "plan a trip to celebrate the end of the six-week transition period." Well, that's an interesting one. Tell me about it.

Sue: We have been so blessed by the changes in our lives that we wanted to mark them in some way that would be the climax of all the rest. So we decided to take a weekend trip to the mountains just by ourselves. Mom was delighted to have the children stay in her home during the time we will be away. You see, we've never allowed her to have them alone overnight before. So we're accomplishing a couple of things at once.

Pastor: Sounds like a good idea to me. Always fine to double up on good deeds. Where are you going?

Sue: To a place up in the Maggie Valley area of North Carolina. We both like that country, and there are a number of things to do there. But mostly, we'll just spend time being alone.

Pastor: Great! You've done some admirable things. But what is this? For week number four you say, "Deal with the animal issue." I don't understand that. Fill me in, please. As the result of that conference, you say, "Buy a dog for the children, but not a large one." Tell me about it.

Bert: The kids want a dog, we're not too happy about that. So we debated the issue at length. Finally, after considerable discussion, we decided to get one. But then the real debate began – what kind of dog? A large one that would protect the home when I'm at work or a smaller one that would be a doorbell? I wanted the larger one; Sue wanted a Lhasa Apso. We went round and round about it and couldn't reach any conclusion. So, we decided to put the matter before the children. We got pictures of both sorts of dogs – a German Shepherd and Lhasa – and asked them which they liked (not telling them we were letting them make the decision for us). Immediately, they both went for the smaller dog – so Sue won the debate. By the way, we had fun discussing the issue, and never once had hard words over our differences. It was a little tough for me to give in at the end, but I can handle it. We get the dog next week.

Pastor: Now, that's good. What would you have done if the kids had made a split vote?

Sue: Don't know, but I'm sure that we'd have discussed it more until we reached a decision satisfactory to both of us.

Pastor: Okay. Now for week number five: "Decide what to do to show gratitude to God for what He has done for us." Interesting. And the conclusion? Well, look at this: "Donate $2,000 to the church for the purchase of give-away books for counselees." Great idea! Tell me more about it.

Bert: This envelope [which he hands to Greg] contains a thank you note and a check for that amount. We appreciated you lending your books to us, but we thought how much better it would be if you could be able to simply give them to counselees. So we came up with this idea. The church can start a fund, spend the entire check immediately on books – whatever it sees fit to do – with no strings attached except to see that it goes to purchasing give-away books for counselees.

Sue: We did have quite a discussion over the amount of money to give. At various times, it ranged from $100 to $5,000. We finally thought that for us it would be financially proper to give what you hold in your hands. Hope it will be enough!'

Pastor: You can be sure that it will be used judiciously. Thank you for this very thoughtful gift. But, remember, you are giving it to the *Lord* in gratitude for His many gifts to you! Okay, now for the last item: "Bert to take a course in New Testament Greek after he completes the elders training course." Well, I must say, that's a surprise. Tell me all about it.

Bert: Well, I've gotten so much out of that course already that my head is swimming. But as we went along, I began to realize that I could get so much more out of Scripture if I knew something of the original language. I recognize that often a little knowledge is worse than none at all. I know I'll never become a Greek scholar. But I also realized that I am limited in my ability to understand the better commentaries when they talk about aorists, subjunctives and so on. I've come to respect the Bible so much that I don't want to study it superficially the way I've done in the past. So I will enroll in a seminary course.

Sue: I think this is a superb idea! I'm just a bit jealous, of course. I'd like to do the same, but two of us away for a night course twice a week is too much. So we've determined that what Bert learns, he will share with me. I can study and bone up during the children's nap times in the afternoons. Then, Bert and I can study together what he learned in the evenings after they've gone to bed.

Pastor: I can hardly believe it! But I am certainly impressed. Whew! What God began in your lives when He brought you for counseling. You are exhibiting the fact in your marriage that the weld is stronger than before the break. Many people only take marriage seriously when they have to think seriously about it.

Now, I have something to ask you about. Would you give your permission for me to write up our counseling sessions as they have occurred in a book designed to help learn what goes on behind closed counseling doors? There are so many pastors who have had little or no good training in biblical counseling and have never actually seen counseling take place that I think it would help them immensely if they could read about a case from beginning to end. I know this is a lot to ask, but would you think it over? We'd use fictitious names, of course.

Sue: Why don't we discuss it right now and see if we can come to a conclusion? How about it, Bert?

Bert: Sounds a bit scary, but I'm interested. I suppose that it could be an even more lasting gift than the check. What are the downsides to it? Can you think of any?

Sue: Well, in spite of the anonymity the pastor promises, there are some who might recognize us.

Bert: Right. But would that be all that bad? Haven't we already been telling everybody about what's been going on here?

Sue: Yes, but not in such detail. But you're right, it could be a lasting gift after the $2,000 check is spent. I'm for it!

Bert: Me too. Let's go for it. Pastor, how will we go about it?

Pastor: Well, I'll see that everything gets written up, but before publishing it, I'll let you go over it to make sure everything is correct. Of course, it will be a great reminder of how God has transformed your lives.

Sue: Will we receive any royalties if it goes?

Pastor: I'm sure that the publisher will share them between us.

Sue: Good. If you agree, Bert, I suggest we give ours to the book fund. What do you say?

Bert: Couldn't be a better use for it.

Pastor: Generous of you.

Pastor: Now, before you leave, I have something to give you. Here. [Greg hands them a package. Sue unwraps it.]

Sue: Oh! How wonderful!

Bert: Let me see. Ah! What a great idea: you framed our marriage vows for display. What a great idea!

Pastor: Glad you like it. Of course, it has sentimental value, but I hope that it will mean more to you than that. Whenever you find yourselves having problems that are difficult to resolve – and you will – take a look at this and remember your counseling, your commitments to God and to one another, and the new ways you learned for solving problems God's way.

Sue: That's just great! But, pastor, what if we hadn't passed the six-week test?

Pastor: Either way, this little gift would be of value in bringing the biblical teaching and practices you learned to mind. If I had given you the proverbial congratulatory gold watch (don't get any ideas!), that wouldn't have worked out had you failed. But I figured that I couldn't lose with this one.

Sue: It's so hard to think that it has all ended. No, that's not right. As you said before, this is a new beginning. These sessions have meant so much to us it will be hard to think that we will no longer be looking forward to them. But maybe we can direct some others who are having problems to you or some elder in the church for counseling. It's so good to know that you all are here when needed.

Pastor: We could go on this way, but I'm sure it would end up all teary. So let's pray now. [They do. But as they head to the door, both Sue and Bert stop to hug the pastor. Smiling, and talking cheerfully, while giving them half a hug in return, he resumes.] Well, I'm not much of a hugger myself, but on such an auspicious event as this I will gladly endure it! [All laughing, they part ways.]

APPENDIX

Some of the More Notable Ways in which Greg Brought this Case to a Successful End

1. Using throw out lines for counselees to grasp that don't influence their answers.
2. Setting up the conference table to be used for various purposes.
3. Asking for lists.
4. Teaching in the counseling milieu while working on problems.
5. Summarizing such teaching at the end.
6. Maintaining consistency in all areas.
7. Using homework and consistently checking up on its performance.
8. Forbidding interrupting and inappropriate speech.
9. Role-playing.
10. Having counselees directing comments to the counselor rather than another counselee.
11. Using a special session.
12. Providing for six-week checkups.
13. Stressing the fact that genuine works flow from true beliefs.
14. Going around the "pie." (i.e., making certain that all major problem areas have been discussed.)
15. Assigning a chapter of Proverbs a day.
16. Calling attention to noticeable terms frequently used and employing a conundrum.
17. Setting and discussing goals and when termination will take place.
18. Challenging erroneous terminology.

19. Surprising counselees with unexpected responses that make them think.
20. Beginning to bring about change in small, single-stranded areas.
21. Calling for action by a counselee unknown to the other counselee to see if he/she recognizes it.
22. Using reading materials to keep from long, detailed discussions in sessions.
23. Probing for information.
24. Requesting a filling out of the PDI.
25. Making use of the important agenda column on the Weekly Counseling Record.
26. Beginning counseling by discussing the basic questions on the PDI.
27. "Playing off" of counselee words and comments (e.g., "magic").
28. Applying God's promises to the counselees' circumstances.
29. Building confidence and expectation by looking ahead to specific things to come.
30. Basing hope on Scriptural promises.
31. Setting up rules for speaking, homework, etc., from the very beginning.
32. Taking control of sessions.
33. Noticing small indications of progress (e.g., tenderness in Sue's prayer).
34. Encouraging counselee's stated interest in Proverbs (e.g., quoting verses).
35. Making a point of the language of exaggeration (e.g., "always").
36. Establishing Scripture as the standard for truth and action.

37. Avoiding lecturing and sermonizing (e.g., no sermon on headship), yet teaching.

38. Dealing with objections and questions straightforwardly.

39. Agreeing with protests of inability, but saying God enables them to do the appropriate action.

40. Avoiding "pushing" counselees before appropriate time to make commitments.

41. Allowing no sessions to drag; keeping them moving forward.

42. Turning job failure into opportunity to learn, grow, help solve marriage problems.

43. Stressing the place of God's providential moving for good in untoward circumstances.

44. Insisting that God's Word is more "realistic" than human ideas.

45. Showing considerable flexibility.

46. Setting forth specific instructions for job-hunting.

47. Turning comment about "thrown out" of session into a plug for homework.

48. Playing off terms such as "civil engineer" as a mnemonic device.

49. Forbidding gossip, name-calling, unwholesome language, and interruptions in sessions.

50. Showing how we are responsible for emotions (e.g., "galling, bugging").

51. Complimenting counselees about genuine achievements.

52. Organizing sessions.

53. Clarifying matters about which counselees are confused.

54. Explaining terms biblically (e.g., "success").

55. Holding forth high biblical objectives and standards and not deviating from them.

56. Stressing that "doing" is first of all to please the Lord.

57. Using the question, "What could you have done differently?" to capitalize on failures.

58. Distinguishing things that differ (e.g., "counting to ten" vs. "considering biblically").

59. Emphasizing incompatibility in biblical terms.

60. Noticing "halo data" or body language

61. Encouraging a counselee to stick to his guns when difficult to do so because it is right to do so.

62. Staying cool-headed enough to give Bert an important assignment in the crisis as Sue leaves.

63. Using offhand statements as teaching opportunities (e.g., comment on self-esteem).

64. Using the church bookstore as a resource.

65. Noticing hopeful changes (e.g., Sue doesn't react to questioning Bible studies).

66. Beginning to signal that the end of counseling is imminent.

67. Distinguishing giving from giving *up* and giving *in*.

68. Handing out printed materials (e.g., rules for conference table).

69. Distinguishing faith in self from faith in God's promises.

70. Contrasting the need for obedience with the supposed need for more faith.

71. Surprising with comments that the work they thought was "good" was actually "bad" (e.g., 16 rules).

72. Helping with failed homework so as to enable counselees to succeed.

73. Quoting, explaining, and applying basic Scripture (e.g., Genesis 2:24).

74. Suggesting an additional session with Bert's mother.
75. Censuring Sue about her suspicions as unloving thinking and attitude.
76. Allowing himself to be touched (Greg "sniffles").
77. Agreeing to unusual requests (e.g., repeating marriage vows anew).
78. Indicating to counselees the signs of authentic breakthrough.
79. Warning, encouraging, and explaining about "going it alone."
80. Summarizing for clarity and retention (and listing summary in writing).
81. Suggesting aids to memory (e.g., note on mirror).
82. Surprising Bert by showing him love is a man's responsibility.
83. Springing on counselees that counseling has ended, yet transition has begun.
84. Making transition the alternative to termination.
85. Letting counselees know that a good report will be sent to Bert's boss.
86. Climaxing counseling with the gift of framed vows.
87. Encouraging difficult tasks (e.g., learning NT Greek).
88. Knowing when to cut counseling short.
89. Suggesting how to deal with "Mom."
90. Coming up with the idea of publishing the book.
91. Using well-known phrases to summarize (e.g., weld stronger than before break).
92. Avoiding unnecessary emotion that would cloud discussion.
93. Focusing on God's goodness rather than sentiment.
94. Bringing you, the reader, into the discussion from time to time.

95. Dealing firmly with irrational behavior.
96. Bypassing matters not pertinent at the moment.
97. Explaining success and failure in God's terms.
98. Setting the tone of sessions in greetings at the outset.
99. Offering mini-sermons (e.g., on love, self-love, the basic incompatibility of all sinners).
100. Noting little things (e.g., Bert "saving" Sue from making a wrong statement.)